AF321667

A CONVERGENCE OF CIVILIZATIONS

YOUSSEF COURBAGE & EMMANUEL TODD

TRANSLATED BY GEORGE HOLOCH

A CONVERGENCE OF CIVILIZATIONS

THE TRANSFORMATION OF
MUSLIM SOCIETIES AROUND THE WORLD

COLUMBIA UNIVERSITY PRESS   *New York*

Columbia University Press wishes to express its appreciation for assistance given by the government of France through the Ministère de la Culture in the preparation of this translation.

Columbia University Press
Publishers Since 1893
New York   Chichester, West Sussex

Copyright © 2007 Editions du Seuil and La République des Idées
Translation copyright © 2011 Columbia University Press
All rights reserved

Library of Congress Cataloging-in-Publication Data
Courbage, Youssef.
    [Rendez-vous des civilisations. English]
    A convergence of civilizations : the transformation of Muslim societies around the world /
Youssef Courbage and Emmanuel Todd ; translated by George Holoch.
        p.   cm.
    Includes bibliographical references.
    ISBN 978-0-231-15002-6 (cloth)—ISBN 978-0-231-15003-3 (pbk.)—
    ISBN 978-0-231-52746-0 (ebook)
    1. Islamic countries—Population.   2. Demography.   I. Todd, Emmanuel, 1951–
II. Holoch, George.   III. Title.
    HB3660.5.A3C6813 2011
    304.60917'67—dc22
                                                                        2010042554

CONTENTS

LIST OF FIGURES AND TABLES

FIGURES

TABLES

CLASH OF CIVILIZATIONS OR UNIVERSAL HISTORY?

IT HAS BECOME A COMMONPLACE EXERCISE TO PRESENT ISLAM as a religion that is resistant to modernity. Occasional theologians also consider the life of Muhammad and the text of the Koran to locate the causes of the irremediable mental and cultural obstacles that, in their view, affect the Muslim world. For this scholarship of a new kind, Islamic fundamentalism is the expression of an essential antagonism between Islam and the West.

This essay will demonstrate the superficiality of these pessimistic and aggressive analyses. It intends to provide a different understanding of the world and its evolution. The "clash of civilizations" will not take place. Consideration of profound social and historical indicators points rather to the idea of a "meeting of civilizations."

To demonstrate this we will mobilize the tools of demographic analysis on a large scale. They reveal not a divergence but a wide and rapid convergence of models. The Muslim world has embarked on the demographic, cultural, and mental revolution that in the past made possible the development of the regions that are now the most advanced. In its own way, the Muslim world is heading toward the meeting point of a history that is much more universal than is generally admitted.

An observation to begin with: Demographers have seen fertility in the Muslim world collapse over the last thirty years. From 6.8 children per woman in 1975, the average fell to 3.5 in 2005. Rates in various Muslim countries now run from 7.6 children in Niger to 1.7 in Azerbaijan. The fertility rates in Iran and Tunisia are now the same as that in France. Such a reversal has deep cultural and social roots: It is the sign of a disruption of traditional social arrangements. This disruption permeates relations to authority, family structures, ideological terms of reference, the political system, and so on. Birth control is both a symptom and a cause of a major anthropological transformation.

This dynamic is not limited to the Muslim world, but extends to many other regions. Indeed, it is hard to think of any country that will be able in the end to escape from its gravitational pull. It has gradually become one of the fundamental axes of world history that bars a compartmentalized representation of the planet and disqualifies the essentialist view of cultures and religions. This is one of the major lessons of the last thirty years.

When the authors of this book were students, the populations of the Third World seemed launched on unlimited, uncontrollable demographic growth, engendered by a combination of declining mortality and an elevated birth rate. The analysis of the vicious circle linking population growth and economic stagnation was one of the compulsory exercises in social science. Since then, we have seen all continents, and soon will see almost all countries embark on a process of controlling fertility that cannot be explained without the hypothesis of a revolution in ways of thinking, because economic development alone cannot shed light on this change of course.

The explanatory variable that has been most clearly identified by demographers is not the per capita GDP, but the literacy level of women. The correlation coefficient linking the rate of fertility to the level of female literacy is always very high. Since learning to read and write do not appear to be determined by the level of economic development, we have to acknowledge that the historical movement running from literacy to declining fertility reveals an autonomous development of patterns of thought. The elimination of illiteracy, then, points back to a classic conception of universal history, that of the Enlightenment or the nineteenth century, as Condorcet conceived of it in his *Outlines of an Historical View of the Progress of the Human Mind*, or Hegel in his *Lectures on the Philosophy of History*. It has no doubt gone a little out of fashion, but it remains relevant.

The elimination of female illiteracy is, however, not the only conceivable factor in the evolution of patterns of thought. We will have occasion to examine the importance of male literacy, a less orthodox approach, but one that is particularly effective if one is interested in the decline of fertility in the Muslim world.

We will also have occasion to reconsider the role of religion in these changes. Religion is indeed a crucial variable in demography. No religion seems to be in a position to block the demographic revolution, Islam no more than Christianity or Buddhism. But the history of the demographic transition shows the importance of religious crises that usually (probably always) precede a decline in fertility. In the case of the Muslim world, the religious particularities reveal the importance of an internal division in Islam, that between Shiism and the Sunni tradition, just as the division of Christianity between Catholicism and Protestantism was a major factor in the history of Europe.

We shall see, however, that this Shiite-Sunni split is only a first level of explanation. Where significant impediments seem to persist, as in certain Sunni Arab countries, the underlying explanatory variable is not religion but the existence of a particularly strong tradition of the patrilineal family. The patrilineal family arrangements of the Middle East appeared millennia before the warriors of Muhammad, so that the rigidities that in some cases have retarded the final stage of the demographic revolution cannot be attributed to the Koran or to medieval Muslim tradition. The anthropology of family structures provides a better avenue of explanation for some temporary divergences in development than a pseudoscholarly exegesis of the sacred texts. The analysis of family systems also makes it possible to discard certain rigid and anxious interpretations of the relationship between Islam and cultural diversity. To political theologians who warn against the Koran's intent to govern civil as well as religious life, we can show to what an extent the majority of Muslim populations diverge, in their daily and family lives, from the prescriptions of the incarnate word.

Finally, we will leave room for more classic explanatory variables when they appear necessary, notably economic variables. When demographic pressure on the means of subsistence reaches a critical point, it can have an automatic braking effect on fertility. Conversely, oil income, which is so important in the Muslim world, can slow down certain developments because it creates conditions of artificial abundance, with withdrawal effects and demographic acceleration when it collapses. Nor will we overlook an autonomous political dimension of demographic phenomena: from Kosovo to Palestine and Malaysia, conflicts between groups—national, ethnic, or religious, depending on one's theoretical preferences—have opposed Muslim populations to minorities or majorities of other faiths. The tendency of some minorities to defend themselves by means of high fertility rates is a phenomenon that has been observed empirically, and it has to be taken into account.

The diversity of the factors enumerated does not, however, weaken the fundamental mechanism of the demographic transition and the worldwide process of modernization of which it is a part. Our adversaries will answer that this transition does not provide an explanation for the current difficulties of the Muslim world, notably its economic backwardness and its violence. If everything we say is true, shouldn't one expect on the contrary the emergence of peaceful and prosperous societies?

The technological and economic backwardness of the Muslim world cannot be doubted. Its current violence is also an undeniable fact and exhibits certain historically novel aspects, such as suicide attacks perpetrated on an impressive scale. The American invasion of Iraq, however, reminds us that the West is not about to surrender without a struggle its title as world champion mass murderer, established by the Second World War, including the Holocaust and Hiroshima, all without the spiritual and military assistance of Muhammad. But it is nonetheless true that the Muslim world is now producing fundamentalism and violence on a rather large scale.

The question remains of how to interpret these phenomena. Westerners would like to forget that their demographic transitions were also strewn with many disturbances and a good deal of violence. The convulsions we now see taking place in the Muslim world can be understood not as manifestations of a radical otherness, but rather as the classic symptoms of a disorientation characteristic of periods of transition. In countries where that transition is reaching its final phase, the danger zone is generally in the past. But in countries where the transition is still in the early stages, the potential for disturbances is high and it is appropriate to maintain heightened vigilance. This is the case, for example, with today's Pakistan.

The analysis of the process of demographic transition that is now affecting the Muslim world leads to a different understanding of current disorders. For that reason, the analysis is especially useful.

A CONVERGENCE OF CIVILIZATIONS

1/THE MUSLIM COUNTRIES IN THE MOVEMENT OF HISTORY

LEAVING ASIDE THE SOUND AND FURY OF MEDIA COVERAGE, we can define and follow the movement of history in a simple way. The progression of rates of literacy for the planet as a whole provides a vision, both empirical and Hegelian, of an irresistible ascension of the human spirit.[1] Every country, one after the other, marches happily toward a state of universal literacy. This general movement does not match the image of a humanity divided into irreducible if not antagonistic cultures or civilizations. There are gaps, but there are no exceptions, especially no Muslim exception.

Census surveys that distinguish between age groups make it possible to determine the date at which, in any given society, half the men or women between the ages of 20 and 24 know how to read and write, a decisive moment of transformation when the first generation reaches adulthood with a majority of its members literate. The rate of increase accelerated in the twentieth century. One after the other, in all countries, 50 percent of men achieved literacy, followed after variable lengths of time by 50 percent of women.

Muslim or majority Muslim countries (see table 1.1) were not in the front rank. But Turkey passed the level of 50 percent for male literacy around 1932. Jordan and Syria, in the heart of the Arab world, did so, respectively, around 1940 and 1946, coming on either side of China (1942). Women followed, with a little more delay in the case of Jordan (26 years) and Syria (25 years) than in that of China (21 years). On the scale of universal history, these differences are minimal, if not insignificant. The heart of the Arab world was indeed one or two centuries behind northern Europe, but only eight decades behind Mediterranean Europe, seven behind Japan, four behind Russia, and three behind Mexico. Its pace of cultural development was close to that of the most advanced large Indian states, such as West Bengal and Tamil Nadu, and also close to the most populous and most peripheral Muslim state, Indonesia. Malaysia, another representative of outlying Islam, was slightly behind the heart of the Arab world and behind neighboring Indonesia, because men did not pass the decisive threshold of 50 percent until around 1958. In the 1960s, Tunisia, Algeria, Iran, and Egypt reached their point of entry into the world of reading and writing. Morocco and Pakistan did not join them until around 1972. The least advanced portion of the Arab world, represented by Yemen, was close in its pace of educational development to the most backward part of northern India. The threshold was passed only around 1980, as compared to 1975 in Uttar Pradesh, 1976 in Bihar, and 1979 in Rajasthan. Bangladesh, Indian in language but Muslim in religion, did not reach it until around 1988.

If we set aside Indonesia, Malaysia, and Islamized black Africa—though this does represent 35 percent of the Muslim population—the major Muslim countries of the central zone are characterized by relatively low status for women, corresponding to a specific family structure, which will be described in chapter 3. And the overall level of literacy at any given moment is largely conditioned by the status of women. Where they are treated as minors, mothers do not have the authority to raise their children effectively, and the cultural dynamics of the society show the effects of that lack. But one can observe only a slowing, not a blocking effect. Moreover, the status of women explains just as much the backwardness of Confucian and Buddhist China as that of Muslim Jordan and Syria, and the backwardness of Hindu Uttar Pradesh as much as that of Muslim Pakistan and Yemen. In addition, if one considers the sample as a whole, one observes that the average gap between men and women in crossing the threshold is about 25 years for Muslim countries as for the others: This measure of the pace of the elimination of illiteracy does not show any particularity with regard to Islam.

Although family systems—more or less feminist—explain in part the gaps in rates of educational progress, the position in the area of any particular country, its location in reference to centers of global development, also plays a role. Literacy maps—global, regional, or local—always show diffusion through spatial contiguity. The exceptional backwardness of Morocco, Pakistan, Yemen, and Bangladesh is not solely an effect of the status of women: It also has to do with their outlying position in the Muslim world. Until a very recent period, one could explain in the same way the delay in the elimination of illiteracy in Brittany and Portugal, two very feminist if not matriarchal regions, but also outlying ones.

Whatever the context, development studies never omit literacy in the collection of variables supposed to describe the state of relative advancement of a country. But we are still living in the shadow of a dominant conception of history that persists in not seeing that economic lift-off is a consequence rather than a cause of the growth of literacy. Even accomplished historians allow themselves to be taken in, refusing to take into account the fundamental interactions between patterns of thought that are largely independent of economic processes. Living standards, the rate of growth of the gross domestic product, and unemployment can be attached to these interactions, but in a secondary way.

THE GROWTH OF LITERACY AND THE DECLINE IN FERTILITY

After the growth of literacy, the diffusion of birth control is a second fundamental element in the accession to a higher stage of consciousness and development. And once again, the Muslim world is entering universal history, at its pace and following its path, but toward a culminating point that is the same as that of everyone else.

Statistical analysis, combined with the feminist ideology of our time, has led to an emphasis on the primordial role of women. Minimizing their role in birth control would be as absurd as denying their role in the production of children. But refusing to take into account the role of men in diffusing contraception would also be a great absurdity, even though we must accept the modesty of their specifically sexual contribution to the process of human reproduction. Fathers work, sustain the family budget, and are concerned with the education and generally the future of their children. Their attitude toward birth control cannot fail to have significant effects.

The analysis of the correlation between variables at any given moment may mask the role of men. If one compares literacy levels and fertility rates at a recent date, when the elimination of male illiteracy had been completed, one notes that the lack of change in male literacy levels meant that they no longer had a visible statistical effect on fertility.

But if one adopts a dynamic view of the process of modernization, by linking the date of decline in fertility to the date of crossing a threshold of literacy of both men and women, men and women are placed in statistically equivalent positions. The analysis of correlations then sheds more light specifically on the progress of male literacy. Differences between male and female roles can then come to light, and either they are insignificant or they reveal male predominance in procreation decisions.

For the sample as a whole, including Muslim and non-Muslim countries (table 1.1), the correlation is +0.98 between levels of male and female literacy; +0.84 between the progress of male literacy and the decline in fertility; and 0.80 between the progress of female literacy and the decline in fertility. This is a set of very strong correlations.[2] The gap between sexes is of little significance, but does indicate a slight advantage for men. But if one focuses on Muslim countries in the sample alone, the correlation between male literacy and decline in fertility falls to +0.61, a significant but not very strong value. The coefficient linking

TABLE I.I Literacy and Fertility Decline in World History

Non-Muslim Countries

	MALE LITERACY*	FEMALE LITERACY[†]	FERTILITY DECLINE[‡]	GAP 3−I YEARS	GAP 3−2 YEARS
Japan	1850	1900	1920	70	20
Italy	1862	1882	1905	43	23
Spain	1865	1920	1910	45	⁻10
Sri Lanka	1885	1936	1960	75	24
Korea	1895	1940	1960	65	20
Russia	1900	1920	1928	28	8
Mexico	1910	1930	1975	65	45
Colombia	1910	1920	1965	55	45
Thailand	1914	1943	1965	51	22
Brazil	1915	1945	1965	50	20
Peru	1916	1950	1970	54	20
Philippines	1916	1927	1965	49	38
Kerala	1930	1950	1960	30	10
China	1942	1963	1970	28	7
Zambia	1944	1967	1990	46	23
Tamil Nadu	1947	1981	1970	23	⁻11
West Bengal	1949	1987	1975	26	⁻12
Kenya	1955	1972	1977	22	5
Cameroon	1957	1973	1987	30	14
Rwanda	1961	1980	1990	29	10
Punjab	1961	1981	1975	14	⁻6
Laos	1965	1975	1990	25	15
Ivory Coast	1970	1998	1985	15	⁻13
Nepal	1973	1997	1995	22	⁻2
Uttar Pradesh	1975	1997	1995	20	⁻2
Bihar	1976	2002	1995	19	⁻7
Rajasthan	1979	1997	1995	16	⁻2
Benin	1985	2010	1987	2	⁻23

continued

Muslim Countries

	MALE LITERACY*	FEMALE LITERACY[†]	FERTILITY DECLINE[‡]	GAP 3−1 YEARS	GAP 3−2 YEARS
Lebanon	1920	1957	1950	30	⁻7
Turkey	1932	1969	1950	18	⁻19
Indonesia	1938	1962	1970	32	8
Jordan	1940	1966	1985	45	19
Syria	1946	1971	1985	39	14
Libya	1955	1978	1985	30	7
Saudi Arabia	1957	1976	1985	28	9
Algeria	1964	1981	1985	21	4
Iran	1964	1981	1985	21	4
Nigeria	1970	1983	1983	13	0
Morocco	1972	1996	1975	3	⁻21
Pakistan	1972	2002	1990	18	⁻12
Yemen	1980	2006	1995	15	⁻11
Bangladesh	1988	*2015*	1970	-18	⁻45
Senegal	1990	*2010*	1990	0	⁻20
Burkina Faso	2006	*2020*	1990	-16	⁻30
Mali	*2010*	*2020*	1990	-20	⁻30

Sources: Population censuses and demographic surveys providing illiteracy rates by age and sex. Public records, censuses, and surveys for fertility.

Dates in italics are projections.

*Date at which 50 percent of males between 20 and 24 reach literacy.

[†]Date at which 50 percent of females between 20 and 24 reach literacy.

[‡]Date at which women's rate of fertility begins to decline.

female literacy and decline in fertility falls to +0.55, a weak value.[3] In Muslim countries, the role of male literacy, although weaker than elsewhere in the world, nevertheless seems more distinct than that of female literacy: A coefficient of 0.61 explains 37 percent of the variation. In Lebanon, Turkey, Malaysia, Iraq, Egypt, Tunisia, Morocco, Pakistan, and Yemen, fertility declined before women between 20 and 24 reached the 50 percent threshold of literacy, in countries where men had already crossed that threshold. We have already described this specific role of the increasing literacy of men in the Muslim demographic transition in the context of a study of Morocco.[4]

There are also Muslim countries where a majority of both men *and* women had to attain literacy in order for fertility to decline. In Syria and Jordan, the time between the attainment of female literacy and the decline of fertility was even relatively long (14 and 19 years, respectively). In Algeria, Iran, Indonesia, Saudi Arabia, Nigeria, and Mali, the decline followed swiftly after women crossed the literacy threshold.

A disconnection between female literacy and fertility decline can sometimes be observed outside the Muslim world. Late-eighteenth-century France is a very special case, but its importance cannot be minimized insofar as it invented birth control covering an entire society. But the case of Spain should also be noted. In the most recent phase of human history, West Bengal, Tamil Nadu, Bihar, Benin, and Ivory Coast have also followed this model. The acceleration of the demographic transition in these countries was no doubt the result of greatly increased pressure of the population on the means of survival. The decline in mortality that followed World War II brought about an increase in the population that was likely to lead to emergency measures for slowing its growth.

In a few extreme cases, the decline in fertility occurred not only before a majority of women between 20 and 24 achieved literacy, but also before a majority of men did so. In Bangladesh, an extreme case of demographic pressure in a hostile environment, fertility declined before 50 percent of men had attained literacy. These cases are rare and recent, and affect countries where rapid demographic growth has cast the population into a veritable Malthusian trap. But in general, male literacy seems to have been a minimum requirement: In 46 of the 49 countries, regions, or states in our sample, crossing the threshold of 50 percent male literacy preceded the decline in fertility.

Protestant northern Europe exhibited huge gaps, exceeding a century, between the elimination of male and female illiteracy and the decline in fertility. France, in contrast, led by the Paris Basin, seemed to need only the literacy of the men in the northern part of the country to adopt birth control. These extreme phenomena are linked to the pioneering role of the Continent in educational development and demographic modernization.

If we set aside France and the countries of northern Europe, and if we divide the countries in the sample into Muslim and non-Muslim countries—Catholic, Buddhist, Confucian, Hindu, or animist—we can observe in Islamic lands a shorter average time between the attainment of literacy and the decline in fertility.

In the varied subsample ranging from Mediterranean Europe to South America, Asia, and sub-Saharan Africa (28 countries, there is an average gap of 34 years between the date at which men cross the literacy threshold and the decline in fertility. The elimination of female illiteracy on average precedes by only 8 years the demographic shift. But we should never forget that female literacy presupposes and includes male literacy. This temporal telescoping with respect to women indicates primarily the complementarity of male and female roles. It is usually literate couples who decide on contraception together.

For the 21 countries of the Muslim sample, the time between male education and the diffusion of birth control is only 14 years. As for women, literacy of the majority comes on average 9 years after fertility begins to decline.

These gaps need to be explained. The determining power of the educational variable is not absolute: It has happened that fertility has not changed for more than a century after mass literacy was achieved, or that natural reproduction has immediately given way in the face of educational development (of men alone in certain recent extreme cases). Part of the shortening of the time between literacy and contraception in recent decades obviously has to do with the rapid increase of demographic pressure. On a planet whose population has increased from 2.5 to 6.7 billion between 1950 and 2007, a certain number of emergency reactions were to be anticipated in many regions. But there is also a variable involving patterns of thought that is ubiquitous and diverse, powerful but sometimes unpredictable, that helps to explain the time differences: the religious variable. An examination of the demographic history of the last two centuries, however, once again is disappointing for the socio-theologians of the clash of civilizations. Islam, unlike Protestantism and Catholicism, does not seem to be in a position to put up serious resistance to the decline in fertility.

A "DISENCHANTMENT"[5] OF THE MUSLIM WORLD

The phenomenon of religion has an existence independent of the particularities of each set of beliefs. At a deep psychological and social level, Christianity, Buddhism, Hinduism, Islam, and animist religions are the same thing: an interpretation of the world that gives meaning to life and enables men to function properly in the societies into which they have been born. The detailed nature of belief, the kind of divinity, the type of metaphysical salvation foreseen, the moral code, and prohibited behavior can be examined only at a second stage of analysis. There is first of all the fact of believing anything at all beyond what is visible and demonstrable that is common to all religions. Also common to all religions is the social bond established by the shared belief. For the fundamental paradox of religion is that it is always simultaneously individual and collective: It defines a link between the individual and a metaphysical beyond, but an isolated individual is in general incapable of believing in any transcendence at all.

A society equipped with a stable and certain belief system provides its members with a meaning for things and for life. In such a context, reproduction may seem to be natural and necessary. The religions that have survived among large populations by definition transmit a positive vision of procreation: Those that, in contrast, have asserted the meaninglessness of procreation—and they have existed—have been doomed to die out with their adherents. For major religions, whether or not they are universalist, children who come into the world have meaning, as the world itself does. They therefore naturally have a natalist view, although it may be qualified. Christianity manifests a negative attitude toward sexuality, which has sometimes led it to favor celibacy, whose effects are obviously antinatalist. Islam is more tolerant of pleasure and of certain forms of contraception, the practice of which may indeed reduce the birth rate. *Azl*, or *coitus interruptus*, was accepted by Muhammad and, by extension, Islam tolerates all other forms of contraception. But beyond these nuances, the general attitude of all major religions is to encourage reproduction as the application of a divine plan. If God created man, it was not so that he would disappear, but would multiply. These obvious points need to be reiterated before examining what happens when religious belief collapses.

The simplest thing is to proceed historically and empirically by describing the first declines in fertility, which occurred in the context of the European cultural and economic liftoff, beginning in the late eighteenth century. The pioneering country was France, where fertility began to decline in the small towns of the Paris Basin in the twenty years preceding the Revolution. The process was generalized apparently in connection with the political transformation. The total fertility rate fell from 5.5 in the mid-eighteenth century to 4 children per woman around 1830, 3 around 1890, and 2.5 around 1910. On the eve of the Revolution, the Paris Basin belonged in its level of development to northern Europe, but it was far from the most educationally advanced region. Half of young men knew how to read and write, but the proportion of the population that was literate was much higher in Protestant countries such as England, Sweden, Holland, and Prussia. Even Catholic Germany was more culturally advanced. The classic correlation between female literacy and decline in fertility would suggest that fertility decline should have occurred first in northern Europe, which was a pioneer in education. What factor can explain France's precocity? Quite simply, the collapse of religious belief that took place over the half century preceding the Revolution. Beginning in the 1730s and 1740s, the recruitment of priests dried up in the Paris Basin. In northern Europe, Protestant or not, religious belief resisted, as did fertility, for an entire century, despite a distinctly higher educational level.

Religious recruitment and observance started to flag in England and the Netherlands after 1880, and in Sweden and Prussia after 1890. Simultaneously, or with a few years' delay, fertility fell off and Protestant nations began the demographic transition.[6]

Between 1921 and 1930, the fertility rate in England was 2.16; in Germany, 2.20; in Sweden, 2.24; and in France, 2.30. The coincidence between religious collapse and the spread of birth control is striking and unquestionable. It should not be forgotten that crossing a certain threshold of literacy was a necessary condition. In regions such as Andalusia or southern Italy, where religious observance collapsed, as in France, in the second half of the eighteenth century, but where the population remained largely illiterate, fertility did not decline. What the demographic history of Europe reveals is the existence of a twofold determination leading to birth control, two equally necessary conditions: the rise in educational level and the decline in religious observance, two phenomena that were obviously linked but not in a simple or instantaneous way.

A third phase of decisive decline in fertility can be observed in the wake of the postwar baby boom. Although one cannot consider the ebbing of religious observance to be the primary factor producing Europe's currently very low fertility rates, a partial coincidence should once again be noted. Beginning in 1965, Catholic religious observance collapsed where it had remained significant: on the periphery of France, in southern Germany and the Rhineland, in the southern Netherlands and Belgium, in northern Italy, northwestern Spain, northern Portugal, and Quebec. The latest decline in fertility in the Western world occurred in the immediate aftermath of the last religious decline.

Western Europe, Catholic and Protestant, was not the only place where the law making the collapse of religious belief a prerequisite for the decline in fertility applied. In Russia and China, the ebbing of religion seemed to be an immediate consequence of a communist revolution that put atheism at the heart of its metaphysical program. In Russia, the decline in fertility followed very soon after the atheist revolution, around 1928. There was a certain gap in China: The revolution triumphed in 1949 began again with the cultural revolution of 1966–1969, and fertility began to decline in 1970. Significantly, and contrary to the expectations of religious anticommunists, neither Russian Orthodoxy nor the mixture of Buddhism and Confucianism that characterized prerevolutionary China reemerged as powerful forces in the wake of the collapse of communism. Communist antireligious fury was not the cause of the fading of Orthodox faith in Russia, nor of the weakening of the family and Buddhist cults that predominated in China. Rather, the ebbing of religious belief left the field free for the substitute creed of communism. The sequence was faster, the replacement of religion with ideology more instantaneous, but the revolutions of the twentieth century did not deviate fundamentally on this point from the sequence illustrated first by the French Revolution. The decline in religious observance had, in the Paris Basin, preceded by a half century the flowering of the liberal and egalitarian ideology, at first revolutionary and then more peaceably republican. The atheism, deism, and anticlericalism later observed in political struggles were belated formalizations, not the causes of the ebbing of religion.

The case of China takes us out of an area of study that is too narrowly Christian. And the example of Japan suggests a certain universality of the sequence leading from religious crisis to decline in fertility and to political crisis, in an order that may vary. The literacy threshold for Japanese men was crossed around 1850; that for women, around 1900. Fertility declined around 1920. It would be a mistake not to take into consideration the religious, or rather antireligious, aspect of the modernization crisis that Japan experienced in the Meiji period, which began in 1868. The reform movement included a violent anti-Buddhist popular movement that reached a climax in 1871, with the destruction of temples, dismissal of priests, closing of monasteries, and abolition of the parochial system.[7] There were a few peripheral uprisings in the name of the threatened religion. The Shinto that came to the fore at the time adopted some elements of the old cult of nature that had coexisted with Buddhism, the true religion of Japan, but it was primarily a new belief system. One hardly dares call it a religion, considering the intensity of its nationalist component. It is probably more reasonable to judge that the collapse of the Buddhist religion left a void, filled in Japan as in many other countries by the emergence of a substitute nationalist belief system. But it is interesting to observe that this nationalism could adopt the guise of a new religious belief. Atheism was not the only path out of religion. In Japan as in Europe, one of the preconditions for the decline in fertility was a collapse of traditional faith. The residual religious component of Shinto perhaps explains the gap of 50 years between majority male literacy and decline in fertility, and of 20 years between majority female literacy and birth control. But the crisis of Japanese transition is now over and, as in Europe, metaphysical belief is extinct. The Japanese of today are astonishingly similar to Europeans in their religious indifference; they also share with Europeans a very low fertility indicator.

The coincidence in time in the ebbing of religion and the decline in fertility, against a backdrop of mass literacy, is a general phenomenon that seems to have touched the three branches of Christianity—Catholicism, Protestantism, Orthodoxy— and Buddhism—in Japan and China. In France, England, Germany, Russia, Japan, and China, a decline in religious observance preceded the decrease in fertility to very low levels, equal to or lower than 2 children per woman, sometimes 1.5. One might imagine the existence of a universal law, independent of the nature of the religious system, the type of metaphysical representation offered, and the form of salvation promised by any particular belief system. Is the fading of religion a precondition for demographic modernization? But if that precondition is necessary, how are we to interpret fertility levels hovering around 2.5 in Turkey, Morocco, Algeria, Uzbekistan, and Turkmenistan, equal to or lower than 2 in Tunisia, Iran, Azerbaijan, and the Muslim population of Lebanon? More generally, how are we to interpret the rather short average length of time between the achievement of literacy and the decline in fertility noted above for the sample of twenty-one Muslim countries? Islam does not seem to pose an obstacle to demographic transition. Here we are confronted with the necessity of making an interpretive choice, in the end a rather simple one.

We might agree that in Muslim countries, contrary to what one observes in so many places in the world, the ebbing of traditional piety and its hold over behavior is not a necessary precondition for the decline in fertility. To support this interpretation we would have to refer to the greater tolerance of Islam for contraception. In that case, far from validating the stereotype of an Islam resistant to modernity, we would make of it, on the contrary, the only major religion immediately compatible with demographic modernity, without which there is obviously no modernity in the general sense. This conclusion seems excessively bold. It neglects the implicit natalism of all major religious systems.

Another tack, perhaps the only reasonable one, is to agree, beyond current appearances, that Muslim countries in which fertility is declining are also experiencing a massive weakening of their traditional beliefs. De-Christianization enabled the decline of fertility in Europe; the fading of Buddhism preceded the decline of the birth rate in East Asia. Does the decline of fertility in Iran, Azerbaijan, Turkey, Morocco, Algeria, Uzbekistan, and Turkmenistan make it necessary to postulate the existence of de-Islamization? Is it possible that a process of the kind is going on, still masked and so to speak unrecognizable? The hypothesis is a bold one, and it is too soon to assert it, because we do not have sufficient distance from events.

To make it less improbable, we should be clear about the meaning of words. De-Christianization did not take place in a day and it did not imply the disappearance of the signs of religion nor of its characteristic general moral terms of reference. One might today call oneself a Christian and a believer and not follow the Vatican's prescriptions in matters of sexuality, family norms, relations between men and women, or the education of children. De-Christianization was marked by a general withdrawal of belief, but more specifically by the collapse of the system of heteronomy traditionally associated with it that pursued individuals into their bedrooms. Understood in that way, a process of de-Islamization has very probably gotten under way, and demography bears its traces.

Hence, there is no necessary contradiction in the fact that the Muslim world is simultaneously experiencing a movement of secularization, with a secular realm becoming ubiquitous in the daily life of individuals,[8] and a significant resurgence in religious observance: Ramadan, mosque attendance, daily prayer, pilgrimage to Mecca, Omra, and Zakka, and so on. This contrasts with the generation of the 1960s, marked by Nasserism in the Arab countries and comparable forms of secular nationalism in other Muslim countries, such as Iran, Turkey, and Indonesia.

Beyond the spread of religious observance, can our hypothesis also accommodate the Islamist upsurge that has reasserted women's obligation to be modest and more generally the necessity for an increasingly active role of religion in the political and civil life of Muslim societies? The Iranian revolution and the Algerian crisis demonstrated that Islamism could achieve a majority at any particular moment. It is clear that the regimes of Muslim countries, whether authoritarian or liberal, are living under the threat of similar developments, which might become uncontrollable. But what the historical law associating religious crisis with fertility decline strongly suggests is that Islamism is a moment and not the end of history and that what is discernible on the horizon thereafter is the almost certain eventual development of a de-Islamized Muslim world, as there is already a de-Christianized Christian world and a Buddhist counterpart.

Fundamentalism is only a transitory aspect of the weakening of religious belief, the new fragility of which leads to behavior intended to reaffirm it. The coincidence in time of the ebbing of religion and an upsurge of fundamentalism is a classic phenomenon. Challenge to and reaffirmation of the existence of God are the two sides of a single reality, even though the abandonment of traditional belief is the inevitable outcome of metaphysical hesitation. Proportions may vary, but transitional ambivalence is always present. It is not even necessary to travel to find examples. The first true atheism emerged in France among the upper classes in the seventeenth century, often in association with the libertine movement. The scientific revolution—in mathematics and physics— overturned the established view of the world and of life. But the very agents of the revolution, the scientists, struggled against the religious doubt that overcame them. Descartes, the founder of analytic geometry, the self-declared theorist of methodical doubt, had no more pressing task than to *demonstrate* the existence of God. As for Pascal, an even more impressive physicist and mathematician, he was literally ravaged by the religious urgency that led him to propose his fragile wager: Nothing to lose, everything to win by believing in the existence of God. He himself was imprisoned in Jansenist suffering. But the Augustinianism—

salvation through grace—affirmed by the Jansenists was the fundamentalism of a world that had discovered the nonexistence of God in the age of the scientific revolution. One of the constant characteristics of Muslim fundamentalism, noted by all specialists, is the force with which it affects students of the sciences. Bin Laden, an engineer, is in this sense an archetype.

Some decades after Descartes' and Pascal's hesitations, religious observance collapsed among the peasants of the Paris Basin, followed by a decline in fertility. Hence, speculating about the emergence of a secularized Maghreb or Iran is not such a bold extrapolation. The process has not reached its end point, but we can already seriously pose the question of the reality of faith in Muslim regions where fertility has reached or gone below the threshold of 2 children per woman: in Azerbaijan, Iran, Tunisia, the Muslim and Christian communities of Lebanon, and Kabylia.

2/CRISES OF TRANSITION

A population with a literate majority is on the path to modernity. The rise in its educational level opens the way not only to a decline in fertility but also to general economic development. An active population that knows how to read and write is productive. Asia's economic takeoff, a phenomenon whose magnitude has become a major element in the process of globalization, was preceded by a rise in the literacy rate. The men of the Enlightenment had anticipated only that positive sequence of events. But by the end of the nineteenth century, the movement toward modernity had begun to show its dark side. Learning to read and write made populations more knowledgeable and individuals more aware. It was then that troubles of mass consciousness surfaced. In 1897, following many other psychological statisticians, Durkheim analyzed in *Suicide* the greater frequency of the phenomenon in literate populations. In the midst of its economic takeoff, Europe was experiencing a breathtaking increase in men's inclination to kill themselves, before going on to kill each other on a continental scale in World War I. Today it is in China and India that the suicide rate has taken off, as much as the economy.[1] For their part, the suicide rates of Arab societies are among the lowest in the world. But can it be asserted a priori that the multiplication of suicide attempts, clearly a highly socialized form of self-destruction, bears no relation to the underlying increase of voluntary death in rapidly developing societies?

Cultural progress destabilizes populations. We need to have a concrete picture of what a society a majority of whose population is becoming literate looks like: a world in which the sons know how to read but not the fathers. Mass education does not take long to destabilize authority relations within the family. The spread of birth control that follows the rise in educational level undermines traditional relations between men and women, the authority of husbands over wives. Separately or in combination, these shifts in authority produce a general disorientation in society and, frequently, transitory collapses in political authority that can be deadly. In other words, the age of literacy and contraception is also often the age of revolution. The English, French, Russian, and Chinese revolutions provide typical examples of this process.

LITERACY, CONTRACEPTION, REVOLUTION

In 1649, the English Puritan revolution produced, a century and a half before the French Revolution, the beheading of a king, under the military dictatorship of Cromwell. As Lawrence Stone, to whom we owe the law associating literacy and revolution, noted, England had just crossed the threshold of majority literacy.[2]

In the Paris Basin around 1730, the majority of men between the ages of 20 and 24 knew how to read and write. Around 1770, fertility began to decline in the small towns of northern France. And 1789 witnessed the onset of the ideological and political crisis that was to last until the stabilization of the Third Republic.

Russia offers an analogous sequence combining literacy, contraception, and revolution. The threshold of literacy for half the male population was crossed in 1900, and the collapse of the Tsarist regime followed in 1917. The elimination of illiteracy among the majority of women seemed to open the way not only to a decline in fertility, which began around 1920, but to a revolutionary resurgence, even more deadly than the October Revolution and the ensuing civil war: Stalinism. Collectivization and the generalization of forced labor and concentration camps constituted a new revolutionary ordeal for Russia.

The same linkage occurred in China. The threshold of 50 percent male literacy was crossed around 1942, and communism triumphed in 1949. The literacy of the majority of women, achieved around 1963, opened the way not only to a decline in fertility that got under way around 1970 but also to the Cultural Revolution and the delirious Maoism of the years 1966–1979.

These examples are of revolutions that were, of course, bloody, but were able to produce new regimes that were stable over a fairly long period. One might also cite in evidence transitional violence leading to open nihilism. In Germany, the rise in militarism that led to World War I and to Nazism occurred in the context of a first decline in fertility, as did the Japanese fascism and militarism that led to Pearl Harbor.

MUSLIM CRISES OF TRANSITION

The political trajectory of Iran matches fairly closely this general model associating cultural modernization, the collapse of traditional structures of authority, and transitional violence. In this Shiite Muslim country, the threshold of 50 percent of literate young men was crossed around 1964, and the Shah's regime collapsed fifteen years later. By about 1981, 50 percent of young women knew how to read and write, and in 1985, fertility began to decline.

Algeria, a Sunni Muslim country, where a very basic Islamism very different from the egalitarian ideology animating the Iranian revolution ravaged the country from 1992 on, provides an illustration of a different kind. In Algeria, there was no doubt an association between the growth of male literacy, which reached a majority around 1964, and the anticolonial struggle, even though it began in 1956 and was won in 1962.

These variables should not be considered with an eye toward finding too close a coincidence when a question of national emancipation is involved. The conflict between two populations with different languages and customs, one of which dominates the other, plays an accelerating role. The Islamist crisis that came to maturity in 1992 affected only the Algerians and came in the wake of majority female literacy, around 1981. Fertility began to decline in 1985. Terrorism spread during the period of the population's greatest mental destabilization.

In Turkey, the attainment of majority literacy went back to 1932 for men and 1969 for women. The Kemalist revolution, underpinned by strong nationalist sentiment, came shortly before majority male literacy, as in the Algerian revolution. The decline in fertility did not wait for female literacy, because it had begun by 1950. But the period of maximum political instability, which was spread over the years from 1960 to 2000, against a backdrop of extreme right terrorism, with a succession of coups d'état and an Islamist upsurge finally digested by the system, matches the chronology of the model associating literacy, decline in fertility, and transitional political disturbances. Turkey's current stabilization, rather paradoxically, has arrived simultaneously with the coming to power in a consolidated democracy of moderate Islamists who frequently liken themselves to European Christian Democrats. The Kurdish question might, however, stir up violence again, because Kurdistan, which is culturally and demographically very backward, is far from having completed its transition.

The pace of Indonesia's cultural development is very close to that of Turkey. It is not surprising to find that substantial transitional violence and a democratic revolution occurred very recently in the country's history. Majority male literacy was attained in 1938 (6 years after Turkey), before the anticolonial uprising. Female literacy followed in 1962 (7 years before Turkey). The high status of women in Indonesia may explain the greater temporal proximity of male and female literacy in the country. The chronological sequence seemed to lead to a very specific political crisis, as deadly as it was mysterious: the massacre of communists in 1965 and 1966. Fertility began to decline in 1970.

In Lebanon, the so-called civil war, between and within religious denominations (Christians, including Maronites, Sunnis, Shiites, and Druze), extended from 1975 to 1990. Usually seen in Europe as a manifestation of regressive barbarism, this period of unbridled violence occurred simultaneously with the spread to Muslim populations of the decline in fertility that had begun before 1950 among Christians. The violence clearly came after general literacy, which crossed the significant thresholds around 1920 for men and 1957 for women. It is probable that a detailed analysis by religious denomination would reveal a fairly close correspondence between increased literacy among Shiite women and the exacerbation of the civil war.

ISLAMISM AND FORECASTING THE FUTURE

If one recognizes the dark side of the modernization brought forward by literacy, then one is able to understand the past, avoid mistakes in interpreting the present, and even get a grasp on the future. We can identify countries where the transition is under way and entertain the hypothesis of a zone of risk that has not yet been crossed. But we can also sometimes establish the fact that, despite troubling ideological and religious appearances, one or another country has already gone through the zone of maximum risk some time ago and that, although not completely absent, the potential for political disturbances is not as high as is commonly thought.

Countries like Morocco and Pakistan are exhibiting signs of fever, notably a rising Islamist challenge and a higher than average production of terrorists. Indicators of literacy and fertility place these countries in the zone of maximum transitional danger. A majority of women in Morocco did not attain literacy until about 1996; in Pakistan this occurred around 2002. But Morocco benefited, so to speak, from a precocious decline in fertility as early as 1975. This gap had the virtue of spreading out over time the phenomena likely to nourish ideological disorientation. In Pakistan, a notoriously unstable country, the decline in fertility did not begin until around 1990, a short time before the majority of women knew how to read and write. The country now finds itself in the midst of a transition crisis, and major political disturbances could ensue.

Saudi Arabia is one of the group of Arab countries that crossed the literacy threshold some time ago, although the stability of the political regime does not seem to have been fundamentally affected by that fact. Majority literacy was reached well in the past in the kingdom—1957 for men, 1976 for women—and fertility began to fall off about twenty years ago. There is a sense of muffled revolt and an abnormally high number of violent Islamists, but the regime is solid for now. Oil wealth has, of course, created special, even abnormal conditions for the control of power by the upper echelons. But it must be recognized that several other Arab countries, without the benefit of oil wealth, where social privileges derive more traditionally from exploiting the labor of the population, achieved early literacy without any real weakening of the authoritarian character of their governments. The cultural change merely brought about strong Islamist pressure leading to intense repression.

The literacy threshold for men was crossed in Egypt in 1960 and for women in 1988. This happened earlier in Syria (1946 for men, 1971 for women), and still earlier in Jordan (1940 for men, 1966 for women). In these two countries, fertility did not begin to decline until around 1985. In Egypt, an early but not decisive fall occurred in 1965, but the decline did not resume until the late 1980s. None of these countries has yet completed its demographic transition. Further west, in Tunisia, the literacy threshold, crossed by men in 1960 and by women in 1975, produced a sustained decline in fertility beginning in 1965. With 2 children per woman, Tunisia is at the level of France and Iran. Nonetheless, Tunisia still has an authoritarian regime, although of an unusual variety that combines militarism with feminism. The regime has not faced any democratic revolution and it remains similar to its authoritarian cousins in Egypt, Jordan, Syria, and Saudi Arabia.

In all these countries, the transition to modernity does not appear to have led, as in Turkey, Lebanon, Iran, and Algeria, to a destabilization of the ideological system. Considered under threat, these regimes are in reality likely to be stable for a relatively long time. But it cannot be said that this stability is the end of their history, particularly because in four of them the demographic transition cannot be considered complete. A detailed examination of the family systems of these countries and of the most recent demographic movements would make it possible to formulate hypotheses about this delay.

It is therefore not at all necessary to speculate about some particular essence of Islam in order to explain the violence now stirring the Muslim world. That world is disoriented because it is undergoing the shock of the revolution in modes of thought associated with increased literacy and widespread birth control. In a certain number of non-Muslim countries that have experienced similar revolutions, one can observe massive political disturbances, sometimes more intense than anything seen in the Islamic world.

In Rwanda, the 50 percent literacy threshold was crossed by men around 1961 and by women around 1980. Fertility began to decline around 1990. Racist confrontations between Tutsis and Hutus led to a genocide in 1994 of a magnitude comparable to the worst massacres in Europe. But Rwanda is almost entirely Christian, and to our knowledge no one has attributed the Rwanda horror to a particular essence of Christianity.

In Nepal, majority literacy was achieved by men around 1973 and by women around 1997, while fertility began to decline around 1995. Maoist guerilla warfare, however, continued to flourish. It was anachronistic, considering the international collapse of communist ideology, but it coincided perfectly with the pace of the country's mental modernization. Should Hinduism and Buddhism be held jointly responsible for the violence that shook that society?

In Muslim countries, in Rwanda, and in Nepal, the fundamental mistake consists of presenting ideological or religious crises as signs of regression. They are, rather, transition crises during which modernization disorients populations and destabilizes political regimes. In coming years, this mistaken interpretation will probably be extended methodically to the entire African continent—Muslim, Christian, or animist—which is close behind the Arab world in the race for modernization. Observers are already blaming the persistence of tribalism and other archaic phenomena for the confrontations that are really a crisis of modernity. The predominance of Catholicism and Protestantism in the more advanced coastal regions of the Gulf of Guinea are likely to guarantee a significant Christian presence in the coming troubles. This is already the case in Ivory Coast and Nigeria, where ideological agitation is strong on the coast and where literacy is more advanced and the proportion of Christians larger than in the rest of the country. There is, of course, no reason to take any pleasure in these likely disturbances, but they will have the unintended virtue of reducing the moralizing pressure of Europeans and Americans on Islam.

The violence of European history, from the Reformation to World War II, corresponded to the same movement, more spread out in time, of mental modernization. After the wave passes, countries return to calm. They then look with surprise or condescension at those that follow. This erroneous perspective reveals the very low level of historical awareness in Europe and the United States. Our era celebrates memory but practices amnesia.

THE QUESTION OF IDEOLOGICAL CONTENT

Changes in literacy rates and fertility indicators make it possible to define and track the general movement of history empirically, to locate each country in relative time, to define the degree of advancement of various parameters, and to explain the existence of ideological, religious, and political points of fracture. Crises of transition defined in this way, however, have very diverse content. The French, Russian, and Iranian revolutions did not have the same goals and were not based on the same values. The first was liberal, the second totalitarian, and the third religious, unlike the two others that were explicitly against religion. But there is nothing specifically Muslim about this, because the English revolution of 1640—coming out of the Protestant Reformation—like its Iranian counterpart, led to the overthrow of a monarchy in the name of God. The Iranian revolution did share with the French and Russian revolutions an egalitarian dimension, whereas the English revolution resisted the idea of equality. Protestantism, which does not believe in the equality of prospects for salvation, does not have as a postulate the idea of a universal man.

Transition crises can also take on openly inegalitarian and ethnocentric forms, as the examples of Germany, Japan, and Rwanda demonstrate. The notion of transition crisis thus leaves open the question of ideological content, the values violently asserted by disoriented populations. Why do some proclaim equality and the nonexistence of God, others accept God and inequality, and still others, God and equality? Many other combinations are also possible and have been realized in history, from Nazi inegalitarian atheism to the unspeakable Cambodian nihilism.

To understand the origin of these differences, it is necessary to explore the mental structures of various societies in more depth. Analysis of cultural movements does not suffice to understand the crisis. Family structures have to be considered: The value systems that organize them are very diverse, liberal or authoritarian, egalitarian or inegalitarian, favorable or hostile to openness of the group. Depending on what sort of value is activated by the growth of literacy, one kind of crisis of transition or another will rock a culturally emerging country.

3/THE ARAB FAMILY AND THE TRANSITION CRISIS

VERY DIVERSE FAMILY STRUCTURES ORGANIZED THE PEASANT societies of the past. Their differing value systems can explain the variety of the transitions they experienced. The family model of the peasants of the Paris Basin on the eve of the Revolution was nuclear, requiring newlyweds to establish an autonomous household. The necessary dissociation between adult generations presupposed a *liberal* value in relations between parents and children. A fanatically *egalitarian* rule of inheritance, moreover, guaranteed absolute equivalence among children, sons and daughters. The activation of these values by the growth of literacy led very logically to the French Revolution, whose motto "Liberty, Equality" seems to be a formalization of the latent family values of the peasants of the Paris Basin.

In Russia, the traditional peasant family was communitarian, ideally associating the father and his sons. At the time of marriage, daughters were exchanged between family groups. Married sons therefore lived under the authority of a kind of patriarch. When the father died, the sons could continue to live together, but they generally separated relatively quickly, and property was divided equally. Daughters, members of other households, were barred from inheriting. The latent values of this kind of system were *authority* (with adult children remaining within the sphere of paternal power) and *equality* (confined to males). These are the values made evident and expressed in ideological form by the Bolshevik revolution, and its Stalinist successor, after the threshold of 50 percent literacy had been crossed. Communism was authoritarian, putting it mildly, and egalitarian.

The traditional family in China resembled its Russian counterpart, and the status of women was even lower. But the principal ideological implications were the same as in Russia, and communism emerged when the literacy thresholds were crossed.

The French, Russian, and Chinese revolutions had universalism in common. They all had the ambition of being a solution for humanity, not for the French, Russian, or Chinese people alone. The value of equality implies this posture through a largely unconscious mechanism: If brothers are equal, men and peoples are as well.

The traditional family systems of Germany, Japan, and Rwanda included the opposite value, *inequality* between brothers. The family of origin requires the designation of a single successor, generally the eldest son (male primogeniture). Cohabitation with the adult married son suggests the presence of a principle of *authority*. Taken together, the family values of authority and inequality lead, at the time of educational modernization, to the emergence of transitional ideologies favoring the ideas of hierarchy and social and racial stratification. From an ethnic or international perspective, in these countries the concept of universal man is unacceptable: If brothers are unequal, so are men and peoples. The crisis then leads, depending on locality, to the definition of the Jew as subhuman, the assertion of intrinsic Japanese superiority, or the massacre of the Tutsis, who besides defined themselves as a racial aristocracy.

England is a country with nuclear families, like northern France, but its rules of inheritance are hazy. Since at least the sixteenth century, property has been divided freely, allocated in portions when children marry and set up house elsewhere, or distributed freely by will on the parents' death. The underlying English ideology is thus *liberal* and *nonegalitarian*: Brothers are different, as are men and peoples. The absence of *inegalitarianism,* strictly speaking. prevented the emergence in England and the Anglo-Saxon world in general of violent and absolute inegalitarian doctrines in the transition period.

Islam is one of the major universalist religions. It is therefore not surprising to find egalitarian laws of inheritance in the countries where it is the dominant religion. But the rule is not absolute, and countries such as Maylasia and Indonesia have adopted inheritance rules as hazy as those in England. A degree of ideological haziness also characterized the anticommunist crisis in Indonesia in 1965 and 1966.

PATRILINEALISM AND PATRILOCALISM

In the Surah "The Women," the Koran presents a detailed exposition of a rather complex inheritance law essentially egalitarian for sons, with daughters having to accept a half-share. A significant portion of the inheritance must also be distributed to cousins outside the immediate family. The combination of fractions defined by the Koran presupposes a good knowledge of arithmetic. The theologians of secularism are no doubt worried about the compatibility of these Koranic inheritance rules with the laws of the Republic. But we can quickly reassure them on this point, because most actual Muslim societies, from Morocco to Indonesia, do not apply these rules. In the Arab world and Iran, the half-share for daughters is not respected, and sisters are simply excluded from inheriting, as was the case in traditional Russia and China. In Malaysia and Indonesia, both sons and daughters inherit, in practice favoring the matrilineal transmission of property.

There are not just individual particularities in family structure in the Muslim world, but a fundamental diversity. Three major regions can be distinguished. A central zone, studied in this chapter—Arab countries, Iran, Turkey, Pakistan, and Bangladesh—is characterized in varying degrees by a family system based on men and turned inward. To the east, in Indonesia and Malaysia, women have high status. To the south, in black Africa, widespread polygamy in practice guarantees significant female autonomy. These more feminist systems are analyzed in the next chapter.

The development cycle of the traditional Arab family resembles that of Russian and Chinese families. The ideal is also the association of the father and his married sons. This is a patrilineal system in which succession to property in practice is restricted to males. A man joining his wife's family as son-in-law is very rare. The aggregation into complex domestic groups almost always occurs by the newly married couple joining the husband's family. This system is called *patrilocal*.

The 1981 Syrian census presented an analysis of households according to kinship relations. It revealed that sons-in-law as a proportion of the total of sons-in-law and daughters-in-law amounted to only 2.9 percent. This proportion is an indication of *matrilocalism*. There was a slight increase in matrilocalism—though still a small minority—when one moves from rural to urban areas: 1.6 percent in rural areas (or 98.4 percent patrilocal), 5.2 percent in cities (or 94.8 percent patrilocal).

This situation is typical of the central Muslim zone, whether Arab, Iranian, or Pakistani. In Morocco, the 1982 census indicated only 1.5 percent rural matrilocalism and 12.3 percent urban matrilocalism. The 1976 Iranian census showed 3.2 percent rural matrilocalism and 11.3 percent urban matrilocalism. Although slight, these differences between Syria, on the one hand, and Morocco and Iran, on the other, are significant. In Morocco and Iran, the level of matrilocalism rose twice as quickly in urban areas, a sign of a less absolute solidity of the patrilocal principle. In Iran, the slightly higher national level of rural matrilocalism was significant: Some provinces bordering on the Caspian Sea reached 5 percent. We do not have comparable figures for Turkey, but one may imagine that levels are still higher, because in some western provinces women can inherit equally with men.

Significant differences can be detected among countries in the central Arab zone. Even in Syria, provinces with an Alawite population (a Muslim sect officially connected to Shiism but whose Muslim authenticity is sometimes questioned) still practice matrilocalism in a minority of cases, but more frequently than elsewhere: 6.6 percent rural matrilocalism in Tartus and 12.5 percent in Lattakia. Directly to the south in Lebanon, matrilocalism rates reach around 10 percent. But in the provinces of the Syrian interior, such as Aleppo, Rakka, Derra, Hassakeh, and Eir el-Zor, the level of matrilocalism falls below 1 percent, a clear sign of patrilineal obsession.

Data are incomplete, but it seems that the intensity of patrilineal sentiment declines as one moves away from the heart of the Arab world. Iran, Turkey, Morocco, the coastal provinces of Syria, and Lebanon represent a kind of periphery where the patrilineal principle is weakened and traces of a formerly higher status for women survive. The distribution of residual matrilocalism suggests a process of diffusion of the principle of masculine predominance starting from a Middle Eastern center. But it is futile to look for a religious explanation for this expansion. The massive and dense patrilinealism of the Middle East preceded Islamization and even the ethnic origins of the Arab world. It was already detectable in the Mesopotamia of the second millennium B.C. At most, one can judge that the Arab conquest geographically expanded the domain of patrilinealism, notably to the West, along the Mediterranean coast of Africa. The populations of Egypt and the Maghreb were converted to patrilinealism at the same time as they were converted to Islam and then to the Arabic language.

THE SHIITE LAW OF INHERITANCE

Traces of a family system less hostile to women and less favorable to men and male kin in general can sometimes be found in the religious system itself. Shiite Islam is distinct from the Sunni majority not only because of a different conception of the legitimacy of political and religious power, an insistence on the necessity to interpret the divine law, and promotion of the idea of rebellion against a world seen as unjust. The law of inheritance is also a major element of difference: Although it accepts in theory the principle of the half-share of daughters, disadvantaged compared to their brothers, Shiism does not fully recognize the power and rights of the extended male kin group. If there are no sons, daughters inherit everything that does not go to the mother and the grandparents, totally excluding male cousins from succession, in contrast to what is accepted in Sunni areas, where the *asaba* (male kin) has significant rights. "As for the *asaba*, dust in their teeth": This axiom of law clearly encapsulates the Shiite attitude toward the patrilineal principle in the broadest sense.[1]

In a multidenominational country like Lebanon, the coexistence of Sunni and Shiite Islam enables some individuals to juggle inheritance laws. Riad el-Solh, the first prime minister of independent Lebanon, was born Sunni. His children were all daughters, and he chose to convert to Shiism to be able to transmit the bulk of his property to them.

The slightly higher proportion of households with a matrilocal basis that can be found in Iran is thus quite significant. On the eve of the process of modernization, it expressed a distinctly less antifeminist and clannish attitude than the one that prevailed in the Sunni areas of Syria at the same stage of the process. In Alawite areas of Syria, the inclination to favor women was even stronger. But in that instance as well, a religious difference governed or protected a family basis less unfavorable to women.

The coincidence between religious and family variants is, however, never absolute. In Iran, Shiism uniformly covers the areas where Persian and Azeri are spoken. It is the underlying bond that ties the Turkophone Azeris to the Iranian nation. But the Azeri family is more patrilineal and more patrilocal than the central Persian system, with rates of patrilocalism exceeding 98 percent.

ENDOGAMY

The condition of women in Muslim countries is different from what it is in Russian and Chinese families: They are not exchanged between families, but married when possible to a cousin. The ideal "Arab" marriage is union with the *daughter of the father's brother*, that is, the *patrilateral parallel cousin*, in current anthropological terminology. Marriage between their children prolongs and perpetuates solidarity between brothers. But if the ideal female cousin does not exist, the son turns to another first cousin, or a more distant one, and eventually to a nonrelative.

For the system to work it is obviously necessary that the rule of exogamy prohibiting marriage between patrilineal cousins be overridden. Almost absolute in Russia, as in most countries of Christian tradition, in China, the prohibition against the marriage of first cousins concerns only marriages between the children of two brothers; other types are tolerated. The overall frequency of marriage with a cousin on the mother's side or with a daughter of the father's sister never exceeded 10 percent of the total in China. In the Arab world, in contrast, the principle of endogamy has been applied massively, with rates varying between 25 and 40 percent (see table 3.1).

A central Arab zone, including Saudi Arabia, Syria, and Jordan, can be distinguished, in which the proportion of marriages between first cousins is high (between 33 and 36 percent). Oddly, with a rate of 36 percent, Tunisia belongs to this endogamous core, along with Oman (36 percent). But generally, as one moves away from the central zone, the rate decreases slightly: 31 percent in Yemen, 30 in Qatar, 30 in Kuwait, 27 in Algeria, 25 in Egypt, and 25 in Morocco and the United Arab Emirates. Leaving the Arab world does not change the tendency, since Iran has the typically peripheral rate of 25 percent, and Turkey the even lower one of 15. The rate in Bangladesh probably sinks to 10 percent. In Malaysia it probably hovers around 7 or 8 percent, and falls even lower in Indonesia.

On the outer periphery of the Muslim world, there are populations for whom adhesion to Islam does not imply any preference for endogamy. Muslims in Bosnia, Albania, and Kosovo are resolutely exogamous, as are those in Chechnya and Kazakhstan. In the area of the former Soviet Union, Uzbeks and Tajiks follow exogamous practices, but precise statistics are unavailable. For Azeris, most of whom live not in Azerbaijan but in Iran, rates seem to be between 10 and 20 percent, probably closer to the higher figure.

However, in some very peripheral regions, very high levels, higher than those in the central zone, seem to be exceptions to the model of the attenuation of endogamy with the increase in distance from the core of

TABLE 3.1 Rate of Endogamy (%) in Muslim
Countries at the Beginning of the 1990s

Sudan	57
Pakistan	50
Mauritania	40
Tunisia	36
Saudi Arabia	36
Syria	35
Jordan	33
Oman	33
Yemen	31
Qatar	30
Kuwait	30
Algeria	27
Egypt	25
Morocco	25
United Arab Emirates	25
Iran	25
Bahrain	23
Turkey	15
Bangladesh	10

Source: World Fertility Survey, Demographic and Health Surveys, PAPCHILD, PAPFAM, Gulf Surveys, giving proportion of women investigated between the ages of 15 and 49, according to their family connection with their husband.

the Arab world. In Sudan, the proportion reaches 57 percent, 50 in Pakistan, and 40 in Mauritania.

Marriage between cousins is not prescribed by the Koran. As in the case of patrilinealism, it predated Islam and the ethnic origins of the Arab world. But the decrease in level as one moves away from the central zone does suggest that Islam served as a vehicle for the geographical spread of the endogamous practices of the Middle East. It is likely that the model was adopted not for religious reasons but because it was the practice of a prestigious group, the Arabs, bearers of the message of the Koran. They were worth imitating in the conquered regions, both religiously and in all kinds of social habits. The converse Christian attachment to the principle of exogamy was in contrast completely explicit, even obsessive, reiterated in many councils and made a part of canon law.

In Sudan and Mauritania, it seems that Arab, followed by Muslim, endogamy was strengthened by the existing practice of marriage between cousins. The very high level of endogamy among nomadic herders of northern black Africa should be mentioned here. The Fula in particular have levels on the order of 50 percent.

With regard to Pakistan, with an impressive level of 50 percent of marriages between cousins, it is reasonable to hypothesize that an effect was produced by contact with the exogamous cultures of northern India. Endogamy would thus have been an identity marker, a practice defining one group against another. Punjabi-speaking populations living on either side of the border between Pakistan and India are radically endogamous where Islam won out, but completely exogamous in areas of Sikh or Hindu religion.

PSYCHOLOGICAL AND IDEOLOGICAL IMPLICATIONS OF ENDOGAMY

The traditional Arab family is thus *patrilocal* and *endogamous*. It is a closed and warm-hearted system and extraordinarily resistant. Monographs that describe life and sentiments in local communities show the degree to which the system is not experienced as restrictive. The opposite was the case for Russian and Chinese families, large patrilineal and exogamous groups in which relations between parents and children and husbands and wives seems to have been immersed in an atmosphere of permanent psychological violence. The swift disintegration of these family systems in the period of modernization was no doubt the result of their members' perception that their way of life was mutilating. Nothing of the kind happened with the Arab family. Endogamy softens the complex interpersonal relations produced by an extended family system. The daughter-in-law is not a stranger persecuted by her mother-in-law (all exogamous models) or raped by her father-in-law (Russian model), but she begins her married life with the status of niece of her in-laws, who have been among her kin since birth.

Contrary to what one might think, endogamy thus plays a protective role for women. One of the common scourges of exogamous patrilineal systems is female infanticide. In a system built around an aggregation of males, daughters are not worth much. Their fate is to leave in order to ensure the reproduction of other family groups. They are a burden, and if they are too numerous, they are eliminated. The exogamous patrilineal systems of China and northern India exhibit completely abnormal sex ratios:[2] The number of men compared to the number of women is much too high. In the Arab world, daughters are not fated to leave the family, but to stay and marry a cousin and live under the temporary authority of an uncle. This kind of situation is naturally protective, and female infanticide is not an Arab tradition, although patrilinealism and the preference for sons sometimes induces distortions in terms of mortality. Table 3.2 presents an indication of excess female mortality between the ages of 0 and 5. The patrilineal Muslim world shows a bias in favor of males, but it comes nowhere near the intensity one can observe in China and India, particularly in Punjab and Haryana. China's unenviable pre-eminence when it comes to excess female mortality is a recent phenomenon, a paradoxical effect of the decline in fertility. Before birth control, northern India as a whole led the field for anomalous sex ratios. When it dominates thinking, the patrilineal principle demands the production of a male heir. When they begin to limit children, families prefer to eliminate daughters, usually through lack of care. This is why demographic modernization can have the disastrous effect of increasing excessive female child mortality. In Muslim countries, traditional endogamy has a distinctly moderating effect on these practices, as it does on female suicide, the level of which is very high in China, the only country in which more women than men commit suicide.[3] The protective character of the patrilineal and endogamous Arab family largely explains the extreme infrequency of suicide in countries where this anthropological system is dominant. But it is the family structure that integrates and protects the individual. Religion as such has little to do with the low rate of suicide in the central Muslim world.

TABLE 3.2 Index of Excess Female Mortality Between the Ages of 0 and 5 (normal value = 100)

Country	Excess Mortality	Country	Excess Mortality
Punjab	198	Indonesia	111
China	184	Chad	110
Haryana	177	Sudan	110
Uttar Pradesh	143	Nigeria	110
Rajasthan	140	Bangladesh	108
Bihar	135	Kuwait*	108
Maldives	134	Mauritania	108
Kosovo	131	Algeria	108
Turkey	121	Kyrgyzstan	107
Jordan	121	Senegal	106
Azerbaijan	120	Palestine	106
Iran	119	Saudi Arabia	106
Pakistan	119	Lebanon	105
Oman*	118	Djibouti	105
Bahrain*	117	Gambia	105
Libya	116	Somalia	104
Niger	115	Malaysia	103
Burkina Faso	115	Bosnia	102
Qatar*	115	Morocco	102
Albania	114	Guinea-Bissau	101
Uzbekistan	113	Comoros	100
Egypt	113	Guinea	100
Afghanistan	113	Iraq	99
Tunisia	112	Mali	97
Syria	112	United Arab Emirates*	95

Sources: The most recent surveys and censuses. Calculation of excess female mortality according to K. Hill and D. M. Upchurch, "Evidence of Gender Differences in Child Health from the Demographic Health Surveys," *Population and Development Review* 21, 1 (March 1995), 127–51.

* Native population alone

To understand the affection of Arab populations for their own family system, so different from Chinese and Russian resentment, it is also necessary to consider the prevalent type of authority, simultaneously formidable and nonexistent. The authority of the father is a fiction. The regulation of marriage by custom transforms fathers and uncles into passive executors of rules beyond their control. The young man has a right to his female cousin which the uncle can evade only by paying negotiated damages. The reality of the traditional Arab family is not the (potentially sadistic) omnipotence of the father, as in Russia and China, but solidarity among brothers and cousins, a necessarily horizontal system in which the authority of custom finally leaves little room for parental authority.

Protection of the individual by endogamy will probably not resist modernization. One can foresee and sometimes already observe the collapse of the practice. Studies show that endogamy decreases when educational levels rise. In some countries, the overall level has recently declined significantly. In Jordan, the proportion of marriages between first cousins fell from 33 percent in the early 1990s to 26 percent in 2002; in Egypt from 25 to 17.5 percent; and in Algeria from 29 to 22 percent. Among the countries for which we have data enabling us to study developments over time, only Yemen has resisted, with a level of endogamy going from 31 to 33.7 percent between 1992 and 1997. But Yemen is the least advanced country in the Arab world, and its demographic transition has scarcely begun.

THE SHOCK OF MODERNIZATION

The traditional Arab, Iranian, or Pakistani family is patrilineal, patrilocal, and endogamous. It is a system that has great power to integrate individuals, probably the most powerful on the planet. It is therefore experiencing with particular violence the shock of a modernity that has shaken authority relations. The principle of masculine predominance is particularly threatened by increased female literacy and by changes in sexual conduct, even though men have played a significant role in the diffusion of birth control in patrilineal regions. It is therefore not surprising, at the time these countries cross literacy thresholds, and when fertility begins to decline, to observe signs of massive ideological disorientation. Islamism, a transitional ideology, has arisen out of that crisis. Some of its characteristics are absolutely classic, such as egalitarianism, which refers back to the principle of equality among brothers embedded in family structure, as in the cases of the French, Russian, and Chinese revolutions.

Two characteristics, however, give evidence of a specific nostalgia. First is the fixation on women's status. The obsession about the headscarf and modesty indicates the anxiety of populations whose patrilineal principle has been disturbed by increased female education and by contraception. The other is the temporary revival of religious feeling, which contrasts sharply with the anticlericalism of the French Revolution and the militant atheism of the Russian and Chinese revolutions.

In Arab countries and in Iran, modernization has secreted an egalitarian and revolutionary Islamic ideology, but it is an ideology that also includes exaltation of the image of God. If one accepts the hypothesis of a relationship between family and transitional ideology, this is quite normal. Modernization has undermined the traditional Arab and Iranian family, and it will probably end up destroying it. But there was no reason for this movement to be accepted as liberating, because the populations concerned like their family system and experience it as protective and natural. Russian and Chinese peasants in contrast experienced their family system as alienating. In Russia and China, the shock of modernization engendered ideologies that called for an even swifter destruction of their exogamous patrilineal family system. It might be called an acceleration through ideology. In Arab countries and in Iran, the transition crisis has chiefly brought forth a violent nostalgia, a desire to hang on to a beloved system. At the heart of this system, the father is central and abstract, himself dominated by the custom of endogamy that deprives him of real power over his children in the realm of matrimony. The return of religion produced by modernization is a result of this positive relation to the family, to the father, and hence to God. To the falsely authoritarian father of the Arab family corresponds the particularly abstract and not very repressive God of Islam.

4/OTHER MUSLIM WOMEN: EAST ASIA AND SUB-SAHARAN AFRICA

ONE OF THE CLICHÉS MOST FREQUENTLY ASSOCIATED WITH Islam concerns THE status of women, which many consider degraded in that religious system. In Arab countries—Iran, Pakistan, the former Soviet countries of Central Asia, eastern Turkey, Albania, and Kosovo—the Muslim religion does coincide with strongly patrilineal family systems, usually endogamous, but exogamous on the northern edges of the area. To the east and south, however, Islam spread to regions whose family systems cannot be considered antifeminist in any way. In Asia, outside India, Islam is almost systematically associated with matrilocal and sometimes clearly matrilineal systems. This reversal deserves explanation. To the south, in sub-Saharan Africa, mass polygamy, contrary to many stereotypes, ensures female autonomy that is quite distinct from what can be observed in the central Muslim world.

MALAYSIAN AND INDONESIAN MATRILOCALISM

In Malaysia and Indonesia, when families are enlarged by the addition of a young couple, in two thirds of cases the couple lives with the wife's family for a certain period of time, usually until the birth of the first child. This practice can be called temporary co-residence. The kinship system of Malaysia and Java is, however, considered bilateral, because men and women, as in the French system, have equal rights of inheritance. But there are regional ethnic groups in Sumatra that might be called clearly matrilineal, because inheritance is transmitted through women and because levels of matrilocalism can be extremely high. In Aceh, on the northern tip of Sumatra, the site of autonomist disturbances until very recently, the matrilocal rate was 77 percent according to the 1971 census. In the province of West Sumatra, three quarters of whose population are Minangkabau, a dynamic and mobile group, the matrilocal rate was as high as 91 percent. Aceh features large, stable households organized around a mother and her married daughters. Anthropologists frequently study the Minangkabau because of their matrilineal organization. Like that of the Hindu Nayar in Kerala in southern India, this organization produced a peripheral and unstable position for men, often sent to sleep in the mosque in some traditional communities.

The matrilocalism of the Muslim populations of Southeast Asia cannot be attributed to Islam. It is characteristic of a much larger area that includes Burma and Thailand, two countries of Buddhist tradition. On the other hand, matrilineal radicalization, where it exists, certainly has something to do with Islam. The Acehnese and Minangkabau are among the most heavily Islamized groups in Indonesia. Further west, in Sri Lanka, the very small minority of Muslim Tamils is distinguished by matrilineal inheritance and 90 percent matrilocalism, in a Sinhalese population that has a bilateral kinship system (with 60 percent patrilocalism) and a Hindu Tamil population with a patrilineal system (and 85 percent patrilocalism). Beyond India, Islam did not advance through military conquest. Its belated penetration goes back to the period between the thirteenth and seventeenth centuries. It was carried by merchants and adopted without the use of force. Religious belief seems to have been dissociated from the patrilineal Arab kinship system. The contact between a matrilocal population and a patrilineal religion probably produced a legitimist radicalization of matrilocalism, which led to the emergence of a few clearly matrilineal systems. "We adopt your religion, but with us it's not men who count, it's women!" This attitude led the family system beyond what it had been originally. The existence of these matrilineal systems is a harsh rebuke to the socio-theologians who claim, for example, that Islam is incompatible with the French Civil Code. For it is an understatement to say that the Minangkabau, who are devoutly Muslim, take liberties with Koranic inheritance law. In fact, they apply absolutely opposite rules by using women as the vector for the transmission of property. The Muslim Tamils go further in their indifference to the egalitarian rules established by Muhammad, because they follow in addition the rule of primogeniture, which bestows the bulk of the inheritance on the eldest daughter.

THE MASS POLYGAMY OF SUB-SAHARAN AFRICA

Nonspecialists are generally unaware of the opposition between Christianity and Islam on the question of marriage within the family group, even when they sense a tendency in families from North Africa, Pakistan, and Turkey to turn inward. Endogamy is not held against Islam by secular fundamentalists who are worried about the compatibility between the law of Muhammad and French law. It is true that in theory the Republic now authorizes the marriage between cousins, which Catholicism still condemns. But marriage among kin is in practice more of a taboo than ever among populations of Christian origin. The Jewish tradition, although not having as strong a preference for endogamy as the Arab world, authorizes marriage between cousins, and sometimes even "oblique" marriage, between uncle and niece, prohibited by both Koranic law and Catholicism.

The problem of plural wives—the Koran authorizes a maximum of four—is, on the other hand, a classic subject for theological ideologues. Polygamy exists in the Muslim, particularly in the Arab world, although it is a minority practice, rarely affecting 10 percent of women, and usually closer to 5 percent. It is in black Africa that polygamy is really a mass phenomenon, with the proportion of women living in polygamous unions varying between 30 and 55 percent. The presence in France of a large number of immigrants from Mali has introduced a certain confusion between African polygamy and Muslim polygamy, because Mali is both African and Muslim. But mass African polygamy owes nothing to Islam. A consideration of two peripheral countries, Sudan in the east and Mauritania in the west, provides immediate proof. In these two countries a group that is called "Arab" coexists, not always peacefully, with black African populations. In both cases, the level of polygamy of the Arab group is substantially lower than that of the sub-Saharan population. In Mauritania in 2000–2001, the contrast was spectacular, with the Arabs at 4 percent, the Fulani at 27 percent, the Wolof at 33 percent, and the Soninke at 55 percent. In Sudan in 1978–1979, the Northern Province, the most Arab, had a level of polygamy of 9.3 percent, but Darfur, now notorious for war and famine, was at 37.9 percent. The epicenter of polygamy is located in the interior of West Africa, notably in Burkina Faso, which is religiously divided, with a Muslim population of 50 percent. This religious imperfection did not prevent the country from reaching the upper range of 55 percent of women living in polygamous unions in 1998–1999.

Theoretically, Islam accepts polygamy more easily than Christianity does. Christianity is as fiercely attached to monogamy as it is to exogamy. In Africa, statistical evidence sometimes verifies these theoretical assumptions, but not always. In Nigeria, for example, the Islamic northern provinces have levels between 40 and 50 percent of women living in polygamous unions, compared to "only" 30 percent in the Christian-dominated southeast, which is a fine example of the adaptation of Christianity's preference for monogamy to local customs. In Ivory Coast, the Muslims of the north have a level of polygamy of 44.5 percent compared to only 24.7 percent for Christians. But the fact that traditional animists are at 47.5 percent, higher than for Muslims, shows how little African polygamy owes to the supposed laxity of Muhammad. The case of Chad, where Muslim, Christian, and animist populations coexist, is even more instructive because it exhibits the same kind of configuration, with one difference: Although animists have the high level of 51.4 percent, Catholics are distinctly more polygamous than Muslims (46.8 compared to 35.6 percent).

The truth is that Islam advanced in Africa in an anthropological context in which family systems had been established and differentiated long before its arrival. There are patrilineal and matrilineal kinship systems, variable levels of polygamy, and specific statuses for women, sometimes influenced by Islam, but always marginally. So-called Arab marriage, accepting union with any first cousin, but preferably with the father's brother's daughter, is not characteristic of sub-Saharan Africa. It is widely practiced only by the Fulani, nomadic herders of the northern fringe, immediately south of the desert, at a level so much higher than the Arab norm that it probably had an independent origin. It is also characteristic of some sedentary groups in the same area (Soninke in Senegal, Mali, and Mauritania; Songhai in Mali; Hausa in northern Nigeria). In West Africa, marriage is usually either exogamous or characterized by a preference for cross-cousin marriage, that is, between the children of a brother and a sister, a practice that has nothing to do with Islam. Without entering into a detailed historical and anthropological demonstration, it must be admitted that the essential traits of the family systems of West Africa owe little to Islam, at most perhaps a slight reinforcement of the patrilineal principle, a trait largely prior to the Muslim penetration of West Africa, as it was in Mesopotamia.

The status of women characteristic of Muslim Africa has little in common with that of Arab women. Polygamy, even in a strongly patrilineal system, does not assume the closed form of the endogamous patrilinealism of the Arab world.

In European fantasy, a man with several wives is a dominant figure. In theory perhaps. But in reality, a polygamous household aggregates the basic units of a woman and her children. In this complex structure, the man is certainly at the center, but in practice he navigates between women, who enjoy great autonomy. Beyond the appearance of submission to the man, African women, in Muslim as in Christian and animist

TABLE 4.1 Arab and African Polygamy (%)*

ARAB COUNTRIES		BLACK AFRICA	
Jordan 2002	6.8	Chad 1996–97	39.2
Yemen 1997	7.1	Chad: Muslims	35.6
Morocco 2003–2004	4.7	Chad: Catholics	46.8
		Chad: Animists	51.4
BORDER COUNTRIES		Mali 1996–97	44.3
Sudan 1978–79: total	20.2	Burkina Faso 1998–99	54.7
Sudan: Northern Province	9.3	Ivory Coast 1994	36.6
Sudan: Darfur	37.9	Ivory Coast: Catholics	24.7
Mauritania 2000–2001	11.6	Ivory Coast: Muslims	44.5
Mauritania: Arabs	4.0	Ivory Coast: Animists	47.2
Mauritania: Fulani	27.0	Nigeria 1990	40.9
Mauritania: Soninke	55.0	Nigeria Northeast	43.6
Mauritania: Wolof	33.0	Nigeria Northwest	49.7
		Nigeria Southeast	30.4
		Nigeria Southwest	38.4

Sources: Surveys from World Fertility Survey, Demographic and Health Surveys, PAPCHILD, PAPFAM, Gulf Surveys.

*Percentage values are of currently married women between 15 and 49 with one co-wife.

regions, are seldom shut away, although there may be notable differences between patrilineal and Muslim Mali and the Ashanti regions of Ivory Coast, which are matrilineal and Christian or animist (see table 4.1).

UNPRECEDENTED TRANSITION CRISES?

If there is indeed a link between traditional family values and the form taken by the transition crisis, we should be able to foresee, in the Muslim countries of East Asia and sub-Saharan Africa, movements and doctrines other than Muslim fundamentalism. With respect to Malaysia and Indonesia, we know that the essential stage of the crisis has already passed and that it took different forms. These two countries crossed the literacy threshold some time ago. In Malaysia, latent tension between Malays, Chinese, and Indians gave Islam a tinge of national identity politics, in the context of a family system showing little interest in the idea of equality. In Indonesia, the idea of equality is weak for an Islamic religious environment, and it would require a violent distortion of the facts and their interpretation to establish a parallel between the country's ideological history and that of revolutionary Iran. The anticommunist massacres of 1965, military coups, and the recent emergence of democracy seem quite specific, far from any sequences of events observed in the Middle East. In sub-Saharan Africa, the literacy thresholds are being crossed or are on the point of being crossed, but the only region showing strong indications of Islamic fundamentalism is northern Nigeria, where the Hausa population has a model of endogamous marriage close to the Arab model. Beyond that, it will be necessary to predict, or to analyze without preconceptions when transition crises occur, the emerging values and ideological forms. This applies as much to Christian and animist Africa as to Muslim Africa.

5/AT THE HEART OF ISLAM: THE ARAB WORLD

IN THE 1960S, A RENOWNED AMERICAN DEMOGRAPHER BELIEVED he had found evidence of universally high Islamic fertility rates, which showed no significant tendency to decline and would remain higher than those for the followers of other religions.[1] Nearly 97 percent of Arabs are Muslims. Their high rate of fertility was attributed to Islam, a more natalist religion, he believed, than Christianity or Judaism. This approach to the question is now completely outdated.

In the Arab world, fertility rates have been cut in half in a generation, falling from 7.5 to 3.6 children between 1975 and 2005. The total fertility rate for Arab women with higher education, who are increasing in number, now hardly exceeds the replacement threshold of 2.1 and is often at levels below that. Seen from the global south, the decline has been stunning. Seen from the north, however, fertility rates remain much higher than those in the West and the Far East, which range be-

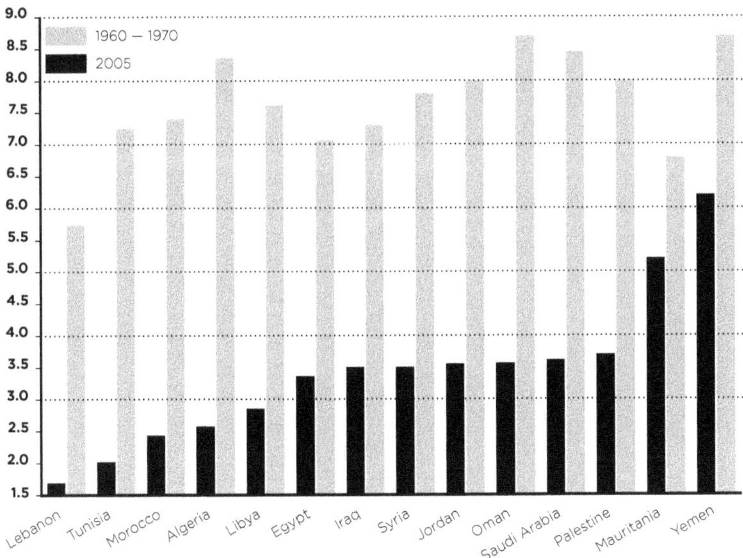

FIGURE 5.1 Total fertility rate of Arab countries before the transition and in 2005. *Sources*: Calculations based on national data from World Fertility Survey, Demographic and Health Surveys, PAPCHILD, PAPFAM, Gulf Surveys, birth registrations, population censuses.

tween 1 and 2 children per woman. In a pretransitional situation, before fertility declined, Arab countries almost all had very high fertility indicators. The norm was 7 or 8 children in Morocco, Iraq, Syria, Saudi Arabia, and Egypt alike.[2]

In two countries, fertility rates were lower than elsewhere. The transition in Lebanon went back to the 1920s. Among Christians, who were then in the majority, the fertility rate reached "only" 5.5 children. This was not because Christian women practiced contraception, essentially prohibited by the Vatican,[3] or abortion, which was also prohibited, but because they married late or never. Further east, in Bahrain, a Western showcase on the Arabian Peninsula, the majority Shiite population had been exposed early on to Western models: The fertility rate was at "only" 6.2 before the transition.

Things have changed. The rate has fallen below the replacement threshold in two countries that in this respect are no different from some European countries. In Lebanon, the number of children per woman is

1.7, barely higher than the British level. In Tunisia, it is 2.0, equal to the French and American level. Other Arab countries are approaching this ceiling of "Western" rates, 2 children per woman: Morocco, with 2.4; Algeria, with 2.6; and oddly, Libya, with 2.9. One bloc of countries has not fallen below 3 children: Egypt, Syria, Jordan, Iraq, Saudi Arabia, and the Emirates.[4] But Yemen, with 6.2 children per woman, is now an isolated latecomer in the Arab world (see fig. 5.1).

A BELATED AND UNEXPECTED TRANSITION: LITERACY AND OIL WEALTH

The demographic transition was later in the Arab world (1985–1990) than it was in Asia and Latin America. A preliminary explanation lies in the slower pace of the growth of literacy. But we also have to explain why most of the Arab world, although levels of literacy were very diverse, entered the phase of demographic transition over a relatively short period. In thirteen out of twenty-two countries, fertility began to decline significantly between 1985 and 1989. This overall movement means that countries such as Syria and Jordan, the most advanced except for Lebanon, had a later transition than their level of literacy would suggest, and that countries such as Morocco and Tunisia moved more rapidly than one would have anticipated from their educational level. In reality, these two countries of the Maghreb began their transition in 1975 and 1965, respectively, that is, even before the more advanced countries farther east. Thus, the disparity in dates of achieving literacy did not prevent the decline in fertility from occurring close in time in all these countries. The economic mechanism of oil wealth makes it possible to explain this paradox.

Arab economies are based more than others on income-producing assets. Not all Arab countries are oil producers, but oil wealth irrigates all Arab economies and, to very varying degrees, all populations, from the richest to the poorest. It makes it possible to raise more children, regardless of income from work. The high level of oil wealth at first neutralized the forces that usually power the transition:[5] not only education, but also decreased mortality, urbanization, the development of an industrial and service economy, and the decline of agriculture. In a second stage, the collapse of oil income sharply diminished family resources throughout the Arab world and provoked a nearly universal fall in fertility throughout the area.

The decline in fertility simultaneously affected two thirds of Arab countries. Exceptionally, the wave swept countries from south to north. The process was unwittingly initiated by the countries of the Arabian Peninsula that seemed to be more important than Egypt. Saudi Arabia and the oil-producing emirates had sowed the seeds of religious conservatism in the form of Muslim fundamentalism, but it is not as well known that they triggered demographic modernization by forcing everyone to end dependence on oil income. Egypt was thus dethroned, even though it was a demographic and cultural giant with 77 million inhabitants in 2007, compared to 34 million for Algeria, 33 million for Morocco, 26 million for Saudi Arabia, 22 million for Yemen, 20 million for Syria, and 6 million for Jordan. From King Farouk to Nasser, Egypt was the primary Arab model. It set the fashion. The "Egyptian" language had become dominant everywhere, so much so that maids in countries as distant as Morocco had begun to speak Egyptian, much to the dismay of their mistresses, who spoke only French. Through its media (the "voice of the Arabs"), television soap operas, and cinema, Egypt had spread a certain image of the modern woman (she was not burdened with a herd of children). Islamism was extremely rare, confined to a few sects. But the first Egyptian demographic revolution, which might have spread through the Arab world, was cut short when Nasser died prematurely in 1970.[6] It ended along with Nasserism, now forgotten, which had been the "contemporary Arab ideology."

With the Arab-Israeli war of 1973 and the quadrupling of oil prices, the once marginal countries Saudi Arabia and the Gulf Emirates became regional powers. Islamism replaced Arabism as ideology. Despite the size of its population, Egypt declined into a second-rank power, dependent on the Arabian Peninsula through transfer payments from several million Egyptian émigrés. This period of high oil income made fertility adjustments less necessary throughout the Arab world.

But between 1980 and 1985 the value of oil exports was reduced by half in the United Arab Emirates and Bahrain, 75 percent in Kuwait, and

87 percent in Saudi Arabia, the most powerful country and host country for the largest number of Arab immigrants. The decline in oil prices and in GDP, closely dependent on them, provoked a collapse of oil-dependent economies and transformed an apparently unchangeable demography. Fertility began to decline between 1985 and 1989 in thirteen Arab countries simultaneously. Numbers declined in Saudi Arabia to 6.5 children per woman from 8.3 ten years earlier. The oil countershock defeated the natalist activism of the Sultanate of Oman, where fertility declined from 8.7 children to 6.65. In Iraq, where the oil wealth mechanism was combined with both an ethnic conflict between Arabs and Kurds and a religious confrontation between Shiites and Sunnis, fertility declined from 7.3 children in 1957 to 5.2 in 1989 (see table 5.1).

The process is simple: Fertility remains high when oil income is enough to maintain it, and it declines when the economy ceases to be dependent entirely on oil wealth.

TABLE 5.1 Period of Triggering of Fertility Transition

Before 1950	1965– 1970	1970– 1975	1975– 1980	1985– 1990	1990– 1995	1995– 2000	2000– 2005
Lebanon	Tunisia	Morocco		Algeria	Oman	Comoros	Palestine
	Egypt 1			Libya		Djibouti	Yemen
				Mauritania			Somalia
				Egypt 2			
				Sudan			
				Syria			
				Iraq			
				Jordan			
				Saudi Arabia			
				Kuwait			
				Arab Emirates			
				Bahrain			
				Qatar			

Sources: Calculations based on national data, World Fertility Survey, Demographic and Health Surveys, PAPCHILD, PAPFAM, Gulf Surveys, birth registrations, population censuses.

But in some countries the fall in oil income occurred roughly at the time the female rate of literacy crossed the threshold of 50 percent. In Egypt half of young women were able to read and write around 1988; in Algeria this occurred around 1981. In Saudi Arabia the threshold was crossed by 1976, or about 10 years before the decline in fertility. Thus, none of these three countries contradicts the most general theory of demographic transition associating female literacy and birth control. It is hardly surprising that Algeria and Egypt, sites of political experimentation during the period of Arab socialism, conform to a standardized image of modernity. But the absolute theoretical "normality" of Saudi Arabia contradicts the stereotype of a country that is fundamentalist in religion and absolutist in politics. However, one cannot claim that Saudi Arabia, so close to Syria and Jordan in its basic anthropological characteristics—patrilinealism, endogamy—would not, like its neighbors, in the absence of a fall in its oil income, have displayed a demographic delay and temporarily maintained a high rate of fertility despite having a majority of literate women.

Oddly, Morocco, one of the least developed countries, anticipated this process. Its unique example had no impact on the Arab world because of its distance from the center. But its entry into the transition period was also the result of exiting from a resource-dependent economy. In Morocco, it was phosphate rather than oil that fostered a demography based on resource income in the 1970s. Despite an official family-planning program launched by Hassan II in 1966, fertility increased rather than declining from its already high levels: from 7.2 children in 1960 to 7.4 in 1973. The tripling of phosphate prices afforded a degree of material comfort that was not very dependent on actual work. But in 1975, the state lost its principal resource, with the fall in phosphate prices at a time when the western Sahara crisis was raising military expenditures. The Moroccan fertility rate declined sharply from 7.4 in 1973 to 5.9 in 1977, following the pace of the increase in fiscal pressure (see fig. 5.2).

A decade ahead of the rest of the Arab world, Morocco turned its back on the traditional separation of male and female economic roles. Between 1960 and 1995 the rate of participation by young women in the

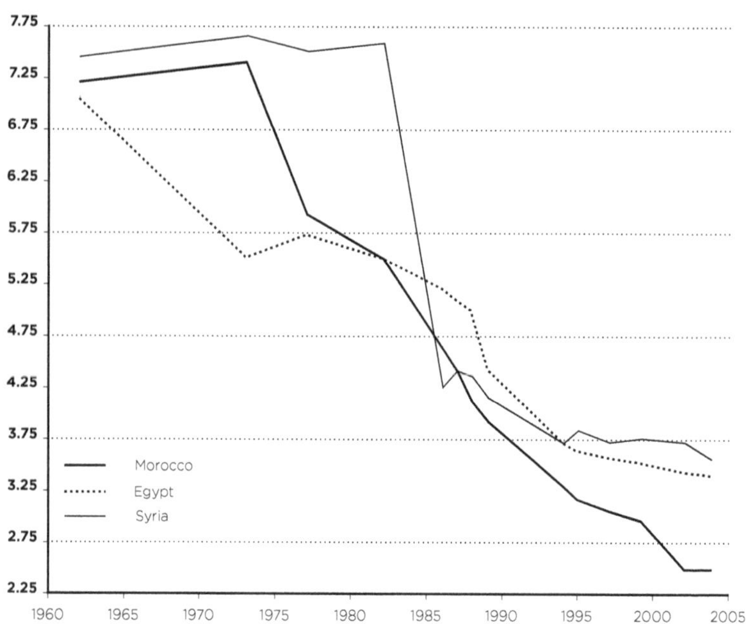

FIGURE 5.2 The advance of the transition in Morocco compared with Egypt and Syria.

Sources: Morocco: Calculations based on World Fertility Survey, Demographic and Health Surveys, PAPCHILD, PAPFAM, population censuses; Egypt: calculations based on birth registrations and population censuses; Syria: calculations based on birth registrations, population censuses, 1960–70, 1982, 1994, and 2004, and World Fertility Survey, PAPCHILD, PAPFAM.

labor force quadrupled, from 10 to 37 percent. New work habits influenced marriage and reproduction by creating new time constraints and a weakening of the family networks that had been responsible for the education of children.

FRANCE AND THE ACCELERATION OF THE TRANSITION IN THE MAGHREB

The most recent fertility rate in Tunisia (2.02) is identical to that of France (2.01). Fertility in Morocco has continued to decline and will be as low as that of Tunisia in less than five years. Algeria, where developments are never simple, saw its fertility decline to 2.38 in 2000, and then it moved up again in 2005. The 10 percent increase is thought to be due to an improvement in security and economic conditions and perhaps to a slight return of the effect of oil income. In Libya, where the sense of identity is complex—Arab, Oriental, Maghrebi, African?—the rate of 2.85 children suggests movement away from the Machrek (Jordan, Lebanon, Syria) and confluence with the Maghreb. Mauritania, on the other hand, is linked more with sub-Saharan Africa than with North Africa. The 2000–2001 survey pointed to a rapid transition and a convergence with its northern neighbors, but for the same years, the 2000 census, which was more exhaustive, moderated this optimism. In 2005, Mauritania's fertility rate (5.20 children) matched that of Africa.

The gap between the Maghreb and the Machrek has increased. Population origins, geography, and colonial and postcolonial history shaped the Maghreb in a specific way that is reflected in its demography. Maghrebi family patterns were influenced by a long period of interdependence: 130 years of life in common between France and Algeria, 75 years in the case of Tunisia, and 44 years for Morocco. To these periods has to be added the half century of interaction since the countries gained independence between 1962 and 1965. Despite indicators of social and cultural development that are often less advanced than those in the Machrek, fertility is lower in the Maghreb and the gap is increasing.

Maghreb identity unquestionably reflects a stronger Western imprint. Media and educational systems, despite their Arabization, have retained a privileged position for European languages, especially French. Textbooks in foreign languages can instill a different way of thinking, even if their substance is identical to that of Arab-language texts. But this factor is very partial. Elsewhere in Africa, elevated levels of French-language schooling have not brought about massive declines in fertility, indicating that teaching in a foreign language is not the only factor involved.

The Maghrebi diaspora in France, Belgium, the Netherlands, and Germany has become the major direct agent for European cultural influence in North Africa. Émigrés contributed to the acceleration of the demographic transition in their countries of origin. In the 1960s, migrants continued to follow the natalist family model. A generation later, values are no longer the same, and emigrants bring home the ideal of the nuclear family. The small distances and the lowering of travel and communications costs have stimulated exchanges. Ironically, at the very time when people are worrying about the penetration into Europe of an irreducible Islam, incompatible with cultures of Christian origin, the real cultural shock was the one experienced by the Maghreb, whose culture was transformed by migration to Europe. In the case of Algeria, where modernization of ways of thinking led to a deadly Islamist crisis, the historical acceleration produced by the interaction with France came at a high price.

Emigration seems therefore to be a capital element in understanding the movement of fertility indicators, which do not depend entirely on endogenous educational and economic factors. The destination point for emigrants is not anodyne. A consideration of Egypt, another major source of emigration, shows that although mass emigration always has an effect, it does not always lead to modernization of thought patterns and the acceleration of the demographic transition. Émigrés from Egypt went almost exclusively to the Arabian Peninsula. According to Gilles Kepel, they brought back a "Wahhabization of the mind." Between 1975 and 1985, Saudi Arabia and the other oil-producing countries contributed to the revival of traditionalism in Egyptian society and, in a country that should have been a driving force behind demographic change, enabled the preference for large families to survive for a longer time. Remittance payments are a practice shared by the Maghreb and Egypt, but their cultural and demographic effects were not identical but contrasting. For the Maghreb, contact established by emigrants with the external world led to acceleration; for Egypt, it led to slowing down.

BACKWARDNESS AND DIVISION IN SYRIA: SUNNIS AND ALAWITES

Fertility in Syria, which remained at record levels until the mid-1980s, began to decline in 1986. Syrians started having fewer children, even in rural areas. This is an example, among many others, of a demographic reaction to the rigors engendered by the decline in oil revenues in the Arab world. Syria is a small producer, but benefits indirectly from the oil wealth of the Gulf states. It is one of the most advanced Arab states in educational terms, because the literacy threshold of 50 percent for men was reached in 1946 and that for women was attained in 1971. The contraction of economic resources occurred in favorable cultural circumstances, and fertility very normally and sharply declined from nearly 7.8 children between 1960 and 1982 to 4.25 by 1990. Thereafter, the rate of decline slowed almost to a halt in the 1990s: 3.50 children per woman in 2005. These uneven developments took place within the framework of an unusually unchanging discourse about demography.

Syria has declared itself to be in favor of a high fertility rate, in contrast to almost all the countries of the global south. Unlike the Egyptian, Tunisian, Jordanian, and even Yemeni regimes, it has never encouraged a lowering of the fertility rate. The "Chinese model" fascinated the government because of its combination of political authoritarianism with economic liberalism. But the birth control encouraged by the Beijing leadership left the leaders in Damascus cold. In official statements as in the conversations of ordinary citizens, the demographic question holds a strong emotional charge.

This natalist credo is a product of the country's complicated history; to understand it we have to go back not just to the Arab-Israeli wars but to the immediate aftermath of World War I. Imagined Syrian territory was much more extensive than Syria's real territory. The *Bilad el-Sham* (Greater Syria), made up of Syria, Lebanon, Jordan, Palestine, Israel, and the sanjak of Alexandretta, was dismembered by the creation of greater Lebanon to the west, the incorporation of the vilayet of Mosul into Iraq to the east, the detachment of Palestine and Transjordan to the south, and the ceding of Alexandretta to Turkey to the north. Natalism was a response to a syndrome of geographical and historical shrinkage. The Arab-Israeli wars accentuated this impulse: Numbers were promoted to the status of a strategic element in a conflict that was expected to go on for a very long time. Nationalism and demography often go hand in hand.

The number of children per woman in Syria was high from the beginning, the wish for children revealed by opinion surveys was strong, and the state did not have to intervene to guarantee a high fertility rate.

Syrians have unanimously preferred large families, ideally 6.1 children in the 1960s and 4.6 children today. Syria is one of the few countries where the ideal number of children is higher than their real number.

We have already encountered birth control policies that failed to transform the behavior of populations that were not yet ready, in Morocco before 1975 under Hassan II and in Egypt after Nasser. In Syria, there was a sharp decline in fertility, even though the regime officially maintained its natalist posture. Moreover, oddly enough, it seems that the regions where the demographic revolution went the furthest, reaching fertility rates between fewer than 2 and 2.5 children are most supportive of the regime. One of the political particularities of Syria is that its extremely authoritarian regime relies fundamentally on religious minorities, chiefly on the Alawites (11 percent of the population), connected to the Shiite branch of Islam, who are dominant in the coastal and mountain provinces of Lattakia and Tartus.

Fertility in the Alawite region was at 2.10 children per women in 2004, the Jebel Druze at 1.80, the Golan at 2.66, and Damascus at 2.45. The Christians (5 percent of the population) scattered throughout the country were at 2 children or fewer. These regions and minority communities might seem threatened by the "explosive" demography of the majority (3.83 children in Aleppo, 5.46 at Rakka, 6.21 at Deir el-Zor), which were two or three times higher. Alone among the large minorities, the Kurds (8 percent of the population) in Hassakeh, on the border with Turkey, are very fertile.

But the government knows it is futile to fight the battle of numbers for its Alawite community of origin and for the communities loyal to the regime. The majority group of Sunni Arabs (72 percent of the population) is undoubtedly a numerical giant. But it is also an artificial category, an aggregation that suits statisticians, although it has no real sociological substance. The other communities are less populous, but they really exist.

The well-known example is that of the two capitals. The opposition between the Sunnis of Damascus and the Sunnis of Aleppo is a part of national folklore and an element in the popular consciousness. The Sunnis of Damascus no longer have anything to do with their coreligionists from Aleppo. In terms of culture (schooling of children, length of time in school), anthropology and demography (family structure, exogamy, mixed marriages, fertility, residential arrangements), and even cuisine, they have moved to the other side, completing the disaggregation of the Sunni group.

Pragmatically, the current regime has adopted a laissez-faire position and tried neither to change community and regional demographic imbalances nor to encourage a specific program for birth control in Sunni regions. It would have been inept to proclaim such a policy and shock religious sensibilities. Why provide an easy argument for opponents like the Muslim Brotherhood who would have been able to claim that the Alawite leaders, heretics if not ungodly, were trying to undermine Islam and weaken Syria by depriving it of its future active population?

What is the explanation for the regional diversity of Syria's demography? The religious variable is obviously relevant, because it provides an explanation for different levels of fertility. It would be tempting to stop at that stage of the analysis and merely assert that Alawite, Druze, Ismaeli, and Christian traditions in this part of the world are not natalist, not preoccupied with increasing and multiplying. A detailed theological analysis would probably end up confirming this hypothesis for the Druze, but not for the Alawites and Christians. It would also be necessary to demonstrate that Sunni Islam is by definition more favorable to procreation. But if we pursue the analysis of social and mental structures, we immediately find a simple and logical explanation not only to the completed demographic transition in Alawite and Druze areas, but also to the slowed and even temporarily halted transition in Sunni regions. It will be recalled from the analysis of Arab and Iranian family structures that the coastal and mountain periphery of Syria is characterized by substantial remnants of matrilocalism, a higher status for women, and greater tolerance for daughters inheriting, a trait associated with the Shiite religious tradition. The interior of Syria, particularly those provinces characterized by very high levels of fertility, are patrilineal to a degree that in global terms can be considered the maximum: Patrilocalism in rural areas is above 99 percent. Inasmuch as this patrilinealism is already attested in the Assyrian period, it can hardly be attributed to Sunni Islam. A direct relationship, however, can be established between absolute patrilinealism and the temporary stalling of demographic change at a level higher than 3 children per woman. Below that level, the probability of not having a son begins to increase significantly. If one has 4 children, the probability of having a son, necessary to apply the patrilineal principle, is 94 percent; if one has 3, 88 percent; and if one has only 2, 75 percent. For fertility to fall below 3 children per woman, one fourth of couples must accept the risk of not having male descendants, which would amount to a renunciation by society of the patrilineal principle. It is easy to understand why Alawite areas, less obsessed by patrilinealism, are not blocked above 3 children per woman.

This problem is not insurmountable for patrilineal societies that, like China and northern India, accept female infanticide. In the Arab world, which for the most part rejects it, the problem is more complicated. It is understandable, then, that there is a waiting period, a final hesitation above that threshold, not only for the Syrian majority, but probably also for countries like Jordan, Saudi Arabia, and Egypt.

THE HETEROGENEITY OF THE ARABIAN PENINSULA

Dominated by two large countries, Yemen (22 million inhabitants) and Saudi Arabia (20 million Saudis and 5.8 million foreigners), the Arabian Peninsula is particularly remarkable for its heterogeneity, because fertility indicators range from 3 to 6 children per woman. But no country has fallen below the level of 3 children per woman, a phenomenon that would signal a radical challenge to the patrilineal norm. Foreigners, whether or not they are Arab, have a large presence in these countries: about three fourths of the population of the United Arab Emirates and Qatar, two thirds in Kuwait, and between a third and a fourth in Saudi Arabia, Oman, and Bahrain.[7] Yemen is the only country for which émigrés exceed immigrants.

This foreign presence may have been a brake on entry into the demographic transition. Saudi Arabia, in particular, would have had every reason to maintain its high fertility rate, because it sees itself as more than merely a Vatican for Islam and would like to see its nationals replace foreigners. Its unlimited oil resources and a certain religious and cultural heterogeneity might encourage the covetousness of poorer and more populous neighbors such as Egypt and Yemen. The dispute with Yemen goes back to 1934. Having lost a war, Yemen was forced to cede the province of Asir to Saudi Arabia. This region is still distinguished from the rest of the Saudi nation by its Yemeni population, its Zaidi religion (a moderate variety of Shiism),[8] and its high level of fertility. Iraq and Iran might have tried to seize the oil wells of al-Hasa, in the eastern part of Saudi Arabia. This coastal region was for a while Shiite but paid for its particularism and high fertility rate with an "impregnation" organized by the government: Sunni immigrants were intended to contain Shiite separatism. Although it is not quite a fortress under siege, Saudi Arabia seems to have a geopolitical interest in the growth of its population. But the decline in the Saudi fertility rate is continuing despite a strong recovery in oil prices: 6.46 children in 1986, 4.37 in 2000, 3.61 in 2005. Insofar as literacy thresholds for men and women have been crossed, the continuation of the transition independently of the price of oil and the level of oil income conforms to the standard theory. But there is a paradox: Conservative, Wahhabi, and natalist Saudi Arabia is accepting the modernization of mores and its formidable implications for the autonomy of women.

These paradoxes of modernity are also found, in an obsessive form, in the five small Gulf Emirates. In addition to their huge weight in the Arab and world economies, Oman, Kuwait, the United Arab Emirates, Bahrain, and Qatar are imposing themselves as new opinion makers, through their satellite television channels that have flooded the Arab world, especially al-Jazeera from Qatar and al-Arabiyya from the United Arab Emirates. They spread an ambiguous message combining conservative Islamism with Westernizing modernism, symbolized by their female anchors, sometimes veiled, sometimes sexy and heavily made up.

The spike in oil prices collectively made these microstates into a new pole of attraction for the elites and the pauperized petits bourgeois of the Machrek and the Maghreb. Foreigners are much more numerous than the native born: 78–80 percent of the population of the United Arab Emirates and Qatar. The native-born population of the five entities together would not fill more than one or two Cairo neighborhoods. As in Saudi Arabia, the factors favoring a high fertility rate—natalism with a national preference, internal rivalries between native or immigrant Sunnis and Shiites—have given way before the effects of modernization. The case of the sultanate of Oman is very significant, because it is the only emirate that may deserve the title of nation-state because of its substantial native population (1.8 million Omanis, 75 percent of the population) and its religious particularity: Alone among the countries of the Arabian Peninsula, it is neither Sunni nor Shiite but Kharijite. Its fertility rate fell after the first oil countershock and is continuing to decline, having reached 3.56 in 2005.

Far from the major centers of world development, Yemen is the demographic dinosaur of the Arab world, with a total fertility rate of 6.20 children per woman.[9] Its low living standards, high infant mortality (75 per thousand), and high rural population (74 percent) are in step, so to speak, with the delay in making the demographic transition, which began only around 1995 and can therefore not be attributed, as elsewhere in the Arab world, to a fall in the price of oil. But considering its literacy levels, the country has not shown any special resistance to birth control. Men crossed the threshold of 50 percent literacy around 1980 and women around 2006. One might even speak of a precocious fertility rate decline, which began in 1995, not waiting for majority female literacy. The 9-year advance in Yemen does not match the 21-year advance in Morocco, where the fertility rate began to decline in 1975, although a majority of women could not read and write until 1996. In contrast to Yemen, Morocco lies completely outside the standard theory of the transition, and in its case it is legitimate to speak of a beginning of birth control depending primarily on majority male literacy, reached in 1972.

Yemen and Morocco represent the southern and western extremities of the Arab world, the farthest from the center, almost equally backward in terms of educational development, because Yemen is only 10 years behind Morocco. Fertility rates of 6.2 and 2.4, respectively, therefore do not measure specific aptitudes, but geographic distance from the centers of modernization. Interactions with Saudi Arabia and France have produced markedly different effects.

A EUROPEAN LEBANON?

Lebanon is the most multidenominational of the Arab countries. It contains four varieties of Islam and a dozen Christian rites. Christians were the largest group until the 1950s, but the country has since become majority Muslim. Despite a general taboo on the question, which explains why no census has been taken since 1932, this fundamental change has escaped no one's notice. Everyone is aware of it, scholars, administrators, and ordinary citizens alike, regardless of religious denomination. But the magnitude of the shift is usually ignored. Differentials in fertility rate and emigration reduced the Maronites, Eastern-rite Catholics, who were the largest group when Greater Lebanon was created at the fall of the Ottoman Empire, from 32.7 percent in 1922 to 19.9 percent in 2005. They ceded preeminence to the Shiites, the proportion of whom grew during the same period from 17.2 to 32 percent.[10] The demographic metamorphosis inevitably affected the political balance. It undermined "political Maronitism," the near monopoly on key government posts by the largest Christian group. It lies behind the 1975–1990 civil war. Lebanon is accustomed to these demographic adjustments, peaceful or violent. Rule over Mount Lebanon in the eighteenth and nineteenth centuries, which the Ottomans had placed under the authority of a Druze emir, gradually passed into the hands of the Maronites, who were then demographically more dynamic than the Druze ,who were numerically stagnant. This stagnation is often attributed to the Druze belief in transmigration of souls: Only an unquestionably Druze soul must enter into the body of a newborn.

The rise in numbers of Shiites, the next stage in the evolution of the balance of denominational forces in Lebanon, may seem to be an irony of history. Volney, who knew late-eighteenth-century Lebanon very well, had predicted their disappearance.[11] If they have grown so much in numbers in two centuries, this is because of a very high fertility rate, which Volney had not anticipated. Until the 1975–1990 war, Shiite women gave birth on average to 8.5 children throughout their reproductive life. This was a record for the region, though perhaps beaten by Israeli ultra-orthodox women. In terms of demographic transition, the delay of

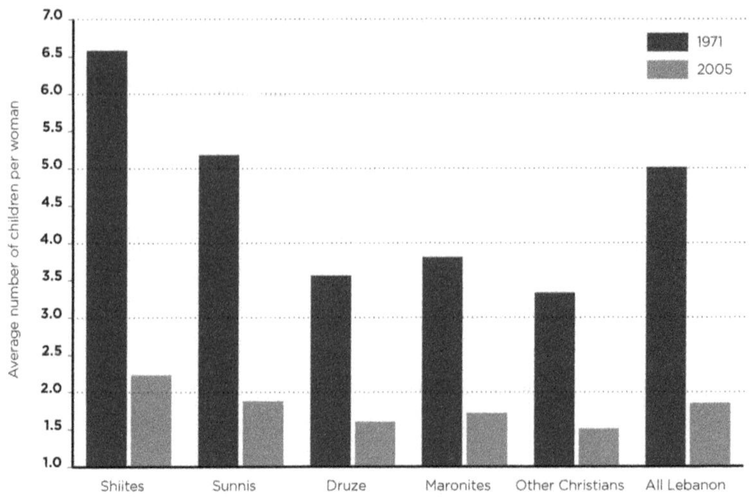

FIGURE 5.3 Decline in the total fertility rate in Lebanese communities, 1971–2005.

Sources: 1971: Calculations based on Lebanese Association for Family Planning, *Al Usra fi Lubnan* (in Arabic, *The Family in Lebanon*), 2 vols. (Beirut, n. d.); 1974–2005: calculations based on Central Administration for Statistics, *A mash al loubnani Isihhat al Ousra* (in Arabic, *Lebanese Survey of Family Health*) (Beirut, 2006), and Central Administration for Statistics, *Living Conditions of Households: The National Survey of Household Living Conditions, 2004* (Beirut, 2006).

Shiites compared to Sunnis (6.9 children), Druze (5.3), and Christians (5.1) was obvious. This excess fertility cannot be given a direct religious interpretation, because Shiites represented and still represent the poorest and least educated group in Lebanon. The delay in their attaining literacy can simultaneously explain the high fertility rate and high mortality that was characteristic of them until recently. But they have not escaped from educational development and the demographic transition. Their fertility rate began to decline around 1975, a phenomenon that helps to explain the violence of the civil war but also makes it possible to glimpse a Lebanon in which communal tensions have been pacified.

It is clear that the war in Lebanon occurred at the decisive moment in the country's demographic transition, when it was destabilized by changes in the relative sizes of communities and when Muslim groups were caught up in a cultural and demographic transformation of great magnitude. Schooling, residence in cities, openness to the media, and the globalization of ways of thinking were no longer the preserve of Christians alone, and this modernization directly affected reproductive behavior (see fig. 5.3). The speed of the transition in fertility between 1971 and 2005 was greater among the Shiites (3.2 percent annual decline) than for all other groups (2.3 percent for Maronites and other Christians, 3 percent for Sunnis). But in Lebanon as elsewhere, the destabilization of modes of thought by progress helps to explain the apparent absurdity of the armed confrontations between 1975 and 1990.

The civil war of 1975–1990 (like the Israeli bombardments of July and August 2006) brought about indiscriminate pauperization among all denominations, which certainly contributed to the adoption of small families.

The convergence was obvious, and at the end of the war, communities seemed to be closer demographically, and perhaps later would be politically. In 2005, the total fertility rate for Shiite women had fallen to 2.2 children, compared to 1.7 for the Maronites. It is not certain that these family choices delighted the leaders of Hezbollah and Amal, who no doubt would have preferred an increase in their electoral or militia base thanks to a kind of Shiite demographic warfare.[12] But political parties and militia machine guns cannot force people to have more children than they want to.

The difference between the two communities now suggests the one that separates France from England. In most other respects they are not very different from one another. Lebanese households are nuclear everywhere, in Shiite as well as Christian regions. Women are heads of household as often in Shiite southern Lebanon as in largely Christian Mount Lebanon. Matrilocalism is even more widespread in southern Lebanon (14 percent in 1997) than in Mount Lebanon (4.3 percent) or majority Sunni north Lebanon (11.3 percent). Throughout the country, marriage is much later than in other Arab countries, and the age gap between spouses is smaller. In this respect as well, Shiite areas manifest a strong inclination for "modernity." Lebanon is not even clearly divided on the question of the choice between exogamy and endogamy, because Christians, unlike those in other countries, are not completely resistant to marriage between first cousins: 10.7 percent in Mount Lebanon in 2001 compared to 20 percent in southern Lebanon. The difference is not insignificant, but even the level in the Shiite region is much lower than that in Syria, where it reaches 35 percent. But fertility remains the indicator that best encapsulates family and mental developments. According to this variable, Lebanon, through all its communities, seems as Western as Europe.

These demographic convergences seem to contradict a political situation that suggests that conflicts between communities could resume. But they are perhaps a harbinger of political and ideological convergences to come. If Shiites join other Lebanese in their demographic behavior, this is because, more than is commonly believed and contrary to what they think themselves, they share the same values. In any event, they are closer to Lebanese Christians, Sunnis, and Druze than to the Syrians, who continue to have 4 children, or Israeli Jews, with 3. The demographic present of Lebanon may predict a "Swiss" political future, an original form of democracy that is communitarian but peaceable and based on negotiation.

THE PALESTINIANS: OCCUPATION, WAR, AND FERTILITY

Palestinians cannot reasonably be studied independently of the state of Israel, whether they are Israeli citizens or residents of the West Bank or Gaza, within an area under Israeli domination. This is not an ordinary region where demographic questions are posed in terms of the balance between population and resources or, more dynamically, in terms of economic development and increased per capita income. In the Israeli sphere, demography cannot be dissociated from a political project that has made the sustained growth of the Jewish population of the country a major strategic objective. The Zionist program is, like the Syrian government, natalist. But there can be no question, as in Syria, of ignoring differences in fertility rates between religious groups. The relative dynamics of the Jewish and Palestinian populations will determine the balance of the state and eventually its capacity to absorb the bulk of the West Bank and Jerusalem. The Palestinians, at the outset one of the most educated of Arab populations, are engaged in a demographic competition that has caused them to substantially deviate from a normal trajectory.

In the developed world, the fertility rate of Israeli Jews represents another anomaly, never before seen in a country with a per capita GDP of $30,000. With 2.60 children per woman in 2005, it seems much less Western than that of various Lebanese communities, Shiites included. It is obviously distinguished from that of Jews of the diaspora, estimated at 1.5 children per woman, which falls within European norms, at the level of the Belgian fertility rate, for example. The fertility of Israeli Jewish women stopped declining in the 1980s. In Jerusalem, the fertility rate for Jewish residents is 3.95. In the Jewish settlements in the West Bank it reaches 4.70 children per woman. This is far removed from Europe's anemic demography. The excess fertility of the settlers is not the effect of ideology alone, or even of religion alone, because it is massively subsidized by direct assistance from the Israeli government. What Palestinians are confronting is an expansionist demography, a demography of combat.

The Palestinians at first seemed effectively protected by the delay in their demographic transition. A high fertility rate placed them at levels that no highly educated population would have been able to challenge. As late as 2005, Israeli Arabs, 1.2 million strong and 17 percent of the population, had a fertility rate of 3.72, one child higher than that of the Jewish population.

In the West Bank and Gaza, the Israeli threat not only temporarily blocked the demographic transition, but produced increased fertility, even among the most educated women. Although already very high in 1985, at 6.4 children per woman despite high levels of education and urbanization, the Palestinian fertility rate increased during the first Intifada (1987–1993). Fertility rates exceeded 7 children beginning in 1988 and culminated at 7.57 in 1990 (8.76 in Gaza). Women had become the guardians of the national borders with the duty of producing the children the nation called for. Yasser Arafat had discovered in their wombs a biological weapon and he exhorted families to have 12 children, 2 for themselves and 10 for the struggle.

Palestinian fertility resisted the paradigm of the demographic transition and the effect of women's education on the number of children. Even after having gone to university, Palestinian women continued to have many children, perhaps not the 12 that Arafat called for, but even so more than 4 on average.[13] An extraordinary thing happened during the first Intifada: The fertility rate began to increase both among the most educated, who were the most politicized, and among the illiterate, who were less politically aware.

The withdrawal of the Israeli settlers from Gaza in 2005 left in dispute the West Bank and East Jerusalem, with a population of 2 million Palestinians and a half-million Israeli settlers, a territory where the demographic confrontation is the essential question. But more recent developments had a surprising result. The second Intifada did not provoke an increase in the fertility rate like the first, but signaled a fall. From 6 children per woman up to 2000, the fertility rate fell to 3.4 in 2002 and 2003. The movement that started with the uprising has continued. It is difficult to imagine the demographic revolution taking place in such natalist conditions, inward-looking and fervent, where religious and political opinion leaders presented procreation as a rampart against Jewish immigration and threatened population transfer. Beginning in 2000, natalist slogans seemed to have lost their effectiveness.

The economic reasons for this are obvious. The blockade of the Palestinian territories and the obstacles to travel have accelerated the decline in living standards. But the decline of the fertility rate goes back to 2000, before the deterioration of economic conditions. Other causes were decisive. Despite the overwhelming presence of the community, families finally started developing for themselves. The decline revealed a divergence between individual and social values. To a large extent Palestinian couples chose to have small families, for the future of their children rather than for the national cause. At 3.4 children in the West Bank, one cannot speak of a completed transition, but of a normalization in relation to regional norms, because that rate is comparable to those of Syria, Jordan, and Egypt.

But in Palestine this development carries a political risk in its wake, because unlike the Palestinians, and contrary to received ideas, the Israelis occupying the West Bank and East Jerusalem have the advantage of a superior demographic dynamic. Their fertility rate has constantly increased, immigration has been sustained, and their mortality is very low despite the Intifada. In 2000, the Palestinian fertility rate fell to 4.18 (3.40 in the West Bank), below that of the Israeli settlers, which was at 4.51. Another cause of concern, with a particular emotional charge, is Jerusalem, the fortieth anniversary of whose "reunification" was loudly celebrated, while at the same time it was feared that it would be captured by the Palestinians of Hamas, not in combat but because of their explosive demography.

It is true that, more than in the rest of the West Bank, resistance to the occupation of Jerusalem in the wake of the 1967 war had involved a high fertility rate. But in 2005, the fertility rate of the 254,000 Palestinians in Jerusalem for the first time fell—by a fraction of a point—below that of the Jews: 3.94 compared to 3.95. Obviously, the mayor of Jerusalem and the national government that followed suit do not read or do not want to read the figures in their latest statistical yearbook.

If one takes Israel and the occupied territories together, one can grasp the absurdity of the demographic confrontations: The high fertility rate of Israeli Arabs is an internal threat to the Jewish state, whereas the high fertility rate of the Jewish settlers threatens Palestinian predominance in the West Bank.

WHEN ONE APPLIES IT TO THE MIDDLE EAST AS A WHOLE THE demographic approach immediately reveals the absurdity or bad faith of Western, specifically American, geopolitical choices. Western democracies, supposed supporters of democratic modernity, refuse to see that the principal center of development in the region is now Iran. The fertility rate of the Islamic Republic, close to 2 children per woman, contrasts not only with the rates of Afghanistan, Pakistan, and Iraq, but also, much more unexpectedly, with that of Turkey, whose membership in the European Union is under discussion in Paris, Berlin, and Brussels.

Among the countries that the American administration has placed in its "greater" Middle East—Turkey, Iran, Afghanistan, Pakistan, and Bangladesh—half a billion souls are not Arab. By themselves, the two countries that formerly made up Pakistan, current Pakistan (165 million) and Bangladesh (147 million), contain as many Muslims as the Arab heart of Islam. With regard to family structure, all these countries are patrilineal and endogamous, although the intensity of the system varies enormously from one country to another. The proportion of marriages between cousins is 8 percent in Bangladesh, 15 percent in Turkey, 25 percent in Iran, and 50 percent in Pakistan. In the westernmost part of Turkey, the family is not completely patrilineal.

During the period of demographic and cultural transition, the temporary revival of Islam brought these societies closer to the Arab world, from which they earlier had seemed intent on distancing themselves. After the fall of the Ottoman Empire, Turkey had snubbed the Arab world and sought to attach itself to Europe. It has again developed an interest in the Middle East, particularly since the Islamists have been in power in Ankara.

The Shah of Iran affected contempt for the Arabs, but the Islamic Republic that succeeded him is present in various ways in Lebanon, Syria, and Iraq. Regardless of national or ethnic susceptibilities, Iran relies on religious solidarity among Shiites, with uneven results. During the 1980–1988 war with Iraq, Teheran failed to win the Arab Shiites to its side, and they remained loyal to Saddam Hussein. But the Islamic Republic did manage to establish a lasting alliance with the Syrian government, the core of which is Alawite, a denomination that was opportunistically considered fully Shiite. In Lebanon, Iran succeeded in setting up Hezbollah, which has become the principal political and military force in the country.

During the Soviet occupation, Afghanistan served as a training ground for Arab Islamists, who later became the "Afghan Arabs." Pakistan was the rear base for these Islamists. Further off, Bangladesh has only economic and migratory relations with the Arab world.

IRAN AHEAD OF TURKEY

Turkey and Iran are today almost at the same point in their demographic transition. Their fertility rates, 2.35 for the former, 2.00 for the latter, are not far apart. But Iran has crossed the symbolic threshold on the way down of 2.1 children per woman.

Decimals are significant. Turkey has presented itself as the good student knocking at the gates of Europe. Iran is the bad boy that has broken ties with the "international community," in anticipation perhaps, like others, of being attacked by America in the name of the defense of democracy and civilization.

In the case of Turkey, a member of the Council of Europe and candidate for entry into the European Union, there is a statistical uncertainty unusual for such an advanced country. Some consider its fertility rate below the replacement level: 1.94 according to the U.S. Census Bureau, lower than the 2.20 proposed by Turkish statisticians. The Population Reference Bureau in the United States accepts the latter figure. The Council of Europe and the United Nations give higher figures, 2.35 and 2.39, respectively. The Turkish demographic transition seems less robust than predicted. The last figures are the accurate ones. The noted

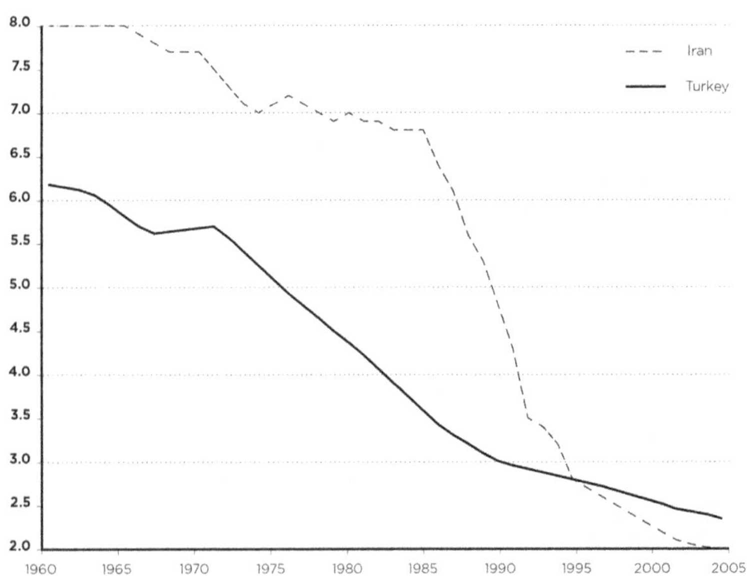

FIGURE 6.1 The transition of the fertility rate in Turkey and Iran (1960–2005).
Sources: Turkey: Calculations based on World Fertility Survey, Demographic and Health Surveys, birth registrations, and population censuses. Iran: Marie Ladier-Fouladi, "Démographie, femme et famille."

American demographer John Bongaarts has no hesitation in classifying Turkey among developing countries where demography is stalling.

But estimates about Iran are in agreement. They make it a distinctly more "European" country: 2.08 according to the U.N., 2.00 according to the Population Reference Bureau, and 1.73 according to the U.S. Census Bureau. French demographers confirm these figures (see fig. 6.1).[1]

THE UNCERTAIN ROLE OF THE STATE

The state has played an equivocal role in these developments. After the bloodbath of World War I, the Turkish Republic ought to have been natalist but it only paid lip-service to the natalist policy. Mustapha Kemal fostered by example a rather Malthusian approach, largely followed by his successors, politicians, high officials, and company managers. The "father of the Turks" in fact had no descendants. The Turkish fertility rate was never very high in comparison to those of its neighbors: 5.5 children for a full fertile life in the interwar period. This moderation was of long standing, in Istanbul as well as in the provinces of the Empire. In the nineteenth century, the fertility rate was higher for Ottoman Christians than for Ottoman Muslims. In moving from Empire to Republic, Turkish society remained fairly Malthusian in its ideals. According to opinion surveys, the desired fertility was lower than the actual one (1.8 children in 1993, 1.9 in 1998, 1.6 in 2003).

In Iran, the actual fertility rate and official policy have almost always been out of step with each other. Despite the Shah's program promoting family planning, the fertility rate of 8 children per woman had been lowered only to 7 by the end of the regime. The remarkable decline that began in 1986 was, contrary to expectations, synchronous with the Islamic Revolution of 1979. For ideological and strategic reasons, Ayatollah Khomeini sought on the contrary to dismantle the shah's family-planning program. Realism and *ijtihad* (interpretation) in the Shiite tradition led the clergy to continue the free distribution of contraceptives in dispensaries and their sale in pharmacies.[2] As in neighboring countries, the fall in the price of oil imposed a rationalization of demographic choices on the population. The crowning point of these developments was the official adoption in 1989 of a second family-planning program, which President Ahmadinejad later found had succeeded too well. In 2007, he railed against the decline of the fertility of Iranian women and against the norm of 2 children per family, perhaps reacting to an interview of one of the authors of this book, who had presented the decline in the fertility rate as a sign of modernization and rapprochement with Europe.[3] Ahmadinejad would like to see an Iran of 120 million inhabitants, 50 million more than now. There is little chance that his advice will be followed by results. There was as little likelihood of this as there had been for recommendations of the former Turkish prime minister and leader of the Islamist party Rafah, Necmettin Erbakan, who had exhorted his people to "have at least 4 children," "because population is the force through which we will establish right in the world. . . . The imitators of the West are trying to decrease our population." The fundamental contradiction of Islamism is that its leaders think of themselves as guardians of a tradition, whereas the popular wave behind them is the result of a modernizing mental revolution. Political victory is inevitably followed by cultural defeat.

Why, contrary to expectations, is Iranian fertility now lower than Turkish fertility? Raw data show that with GDP per capita very close together, Iran is a little more urbanized. The threshold of 50 percent literacy was crossed by Turkish women in 1969 and by Iranian women in 1981. But the Islamic Republic, apparently more culturally dynamic, now has more widespread literacy among its young women, 97 percent compared to 93 percent in Turkey. But all this is only on the surface.

DEMOGRAPHIC TRANSITION AND NATION-STATE

Turkey and Iran are multidenominational and multiethnic. Returning to the practices of the Ottoman era, Turkey, which is 99 percent Muslim, makes no distinctions among the various branches of Islam, unlike Lebanon. But it does distinguish Christians—Armenian, Greek, and Arab—as well as Jews from Muslims. But minority "Muslim" denominations well and truly exist, such as the Alevi, the Bektashi, and the Kizilbas (in all, 20 to 30 percent of the population of Turkey), as do the Dönmeh, Jews converted to islam in the seventeenth century who maintain some religious particularities. The country's ethnic diversity is better known: Kurds represent 20 percent of the population.

Shiite Iran also has its Muslim minorities: 9 percent of the population are Sunnis, but they are not recognized as such. There are also Alevi, Baha'i, and Christian and Zoroastrian communities in the country. Ethnically and linguistically, Iran is even more composite than Turkey, because Persians comprise only 51 percent of the population, with 24 percent Azeris, who speak a Turkic language, and 7 percent Kurds, whose language is, like Persian, Indo-European.

Turkey's past is filled with religious and ethnic conflicts: The Armenian, Greek, Syriac, Alevi, and especially Kurdish questions have not been forgotten and periodically resurface. Before as well as after the Islamic Revolution, Iran has been more serene in this respect.[4] This fundamental difference is reflected demographically. Ethnic and religious rivalries have demographic consequences, just as good relations do. In Turkey, fertility remains marked by ethnicity, because several regions, cut off from the national system, are marking time. In Iran, the demographic transition was more widely disseminated throughout the territory.

An examination of regional demographic indicators reveals the coexistence in Turkey of three distinct demographic phases. A "European" system was propagated in successive waves from two capitals, Istanbul and Ankara. It affected European Turkey and the western part of Asia Minor, the Mediterranean and Black Sea coasts, where the fertility rate is at the replacement threshold of 2.1, and sometimes as low as 1.6. In the center, in Anatolia, the transition is under way and promises to proceed to the end, with rates lower than 3.0. Further east, the Turkish part of Kurdistan is an area with a very high fertility rate. In this Turkish region, bitterly disputed over the course of history, on the borders of Syria, Iraq, Iran, Armenia, and Georgia, the number of children is high, abnormally so if one takes into account socioeconomic and sometimes even educational factors: 5 and sometimes 6 children per woman. The fertility rate is high in the former sanjak of Alexandretta (called Hatay since its annexation by Turkey), which has an Arab population.

These differences in demographic development can be traced back to initial anthropological differences, or at least those existing prior to the transition. In the western part of the country, the status of women was higher and the rate of familial endogamy lower. A division of Turkey into five major zones in 1988 shows a rate of marriage between first cousins of 8.4 percent in the west, and 22.6 percent in the Eastern region, which includes the Kurds. But this rate is distinctly lower than that in neighboring Arab countries such as Syria, which is at 35 percent, but fairly close to that of Iran (around 25 percent). It will be recalled that, before their conversion to Sunni Islam, the Turkish peoples were exogamous, like the Christian populations of the Byzantine Empire, linguistically Turkified after the Ottoman conquest.

The Kurdish demographic particularity can also be observed in northern Syria, in the provinces of Hassakeh and Deir el-Zor, in the suburbs of Aleppo, and in Iraq.[5] Only Iran seems to have avoided this demographic separatism, even though the Kurds are primarily Sunni in a Shiite country. An Iranian province is named Kordestan, although Kurds are also a majority of the population in the provinces of Kermanshah, West Azerbaijan, and Ilam. What is striking when one compares the regional map of the Iranian fertility rate with that of Turkey is the convergence of the Kurdish one with that of other Iranians: 1.9 in Kordestan, 1.8 in Kermanshah and Ilam, and a maximum of 2.5 in West Azerbaijan. In Turkey, the fertility rate in Kurdistan (NTUS 1 region, called "Southeast Anatolia") was still 4.2 children per woman in 2001–2003, compared to 1.8 in developed regions such as Istanbul and the center of the country. Is it possible to speak of a Turkish Republic "one and indivisible" with such marked demographic, social, and cultural cleavages? To discover a fertility rate differentiated by ethnicity in Iran, one has to go to Khuzestan, where there is an Arab minority representing 3 percent of the country's population. But with 2.6 children per woman, this is an Arab population that has crossed below the floor of 3 children and has thus broken ranks with the patrilineal principle. Only the Baluchis in the extreme southeast of Iran on the border with Pakistan represent a substantial difference, with 4.1 children per woman. This group makes up only 2 percent of the total population.

RELIGION, DEMOGRAPHY, DEMOCRACY

The objectivity of demography sometimes forces us to accept a reality that stereotypes and habit encourage us to reject. Turkey is supposed to be modern and democratic because it is the heir, despite the presence of moderate Islamists in power, of a secular, centralist, and perhaps Jacobin tradition. Iran is said to be obscurantist and authoritarian, if not totalitarian, because it is religious. National and regional fertility indicators, however, clearly suggest that Iran is more modern, more homogeneous, and more individualist. But in fact the political indicators that we refused to see were telling us the same thing. Iran is more spontaneously, more naturally democratic. The Turkish regime came out of a military coup d'état with a nationalist tendency, and it has continued to live under the surveillance of the army, which becomes threatening at the slightest sign of deviation. Turkish secularism cannot be identified with the notion of free choice by individuals. In Iran, as in France, England, and the United States, the regime came out of an authentic revolution, and the army does not exist as an autonomous actor. Besides, there are two armies, the regular army and the Pasdaran, who came out of the revolution, a doubling that in practice guarantees the autonomy of the political sphere. Elections are, of course, not entirely free in Iran, because not all candidates can run. But votes are held all the time in the Islamic Republic, and changes of majority are frequent. This is an imperfect but promising democracy, because it is the expression not of a plan from above but of the rebellious and pluralist temperament of the population as a whole.

It is easy to understand why the religious character of the Iranian regime is troubling to the French, whose history has featured the concrete association between secularism and democracy. Anglo-Saxons, on the other hand, have no excuse, because the English Revolution and American democracy both had religious, specifically Protestant, sources. On second thought, French elites have no excuse either. They are supposed to venerate Tocqueville, who demonstrated the link between religious life and democracy in the United Sates in the first half of the nineteenth century. Tocqueville, it is true, did not like Islam, but his knowledge of the religion hardly went beyond Algeria and the Sunni world. Who knows whether better knowledge of Shiism, a religious system propitious to modernity, like Protestantism, would not have led him to qualify his judgment?

Because it brings out the advance of the Islamic Republic, the comparative study of the demography of Turkey and Iran leads to an important conclusion. The fundamental difference in this instance is not that between religion and secularism, but between the Sunni and Shiite variants of Islam. For even before identifying Turkey as the guardian of a secular tradition, we should have identified it as coming under Sunni Islam. This correction of historical perspective does not prevent speculation about an eventual secularization of Iran and the emergence in the country of a secularism with a Shiite tradition.

THE PAKISTANI DEMOGRAPHIC TIME BOMB

The product of two separations, first from India in 1947 and then from Bangladesh in 1971, Pakistan, the "country of the pure," has since then increased in relative demographic mass because of its high fertility rate. At the time of the 1971 partition, the country had 5 million fewer inhabitants than Bangladesh; today it has 18 million more.

Demographic rivalries in the Indian subcontinent do not involve Pakistan and Bangladesh to any great extent. India is the real reference point, the threat that has to be confronted. But with 1.1 billion inhabitants, India cannot be caught, even though its growth has been slower since 1950, with the population multiplied by 3.2, compared to 4.5 in Pakistan. But the fantasy of a return to the golden age of the Mughal Empire, the Muslim dynasty that dominated the subcontinent between 1504 and 1857, has perhaps not completely disappeared. If Islam in the entirety of the Indian subcontinent were unified (Pakistan with Bangladesh and the Indian Muslims), it would be possible to anticipate in the long term that the number of Muslims would catch up with the number of Hindus. Islam in the subcontinent in 2007 already represented a half billion individuals. In terms of potential, it has a distinctly higher fertility rate (see fig. 6.2). Muslims obviously pay for this excess fertility by a relative deterioration in their living standards.

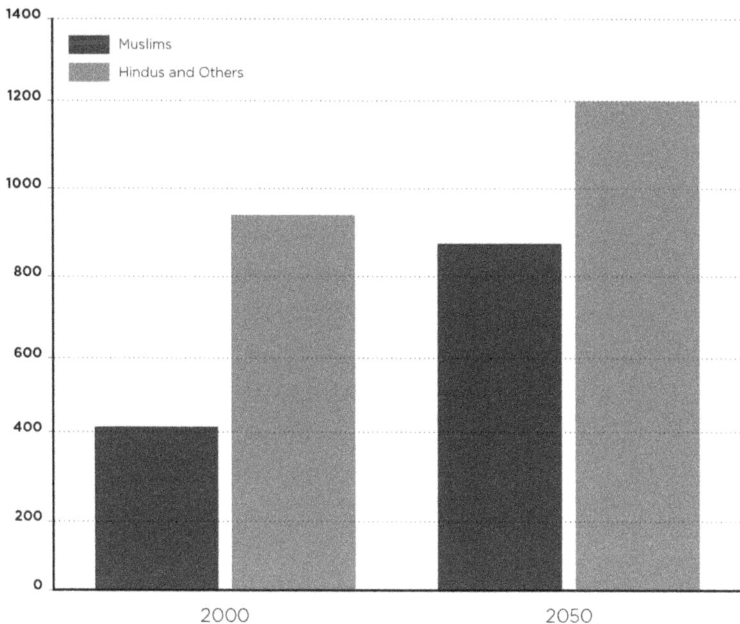

FIGURE 6.2 Muslim and Hindu populations of the Indian subcontinent (India, Pakistan, Bangladesh) in 2000 and predicted for 2050.
Sources: Projection for 2050 based on that for Pakistan and Bangladesh and demographic differentials according to religion in India. Figures on the side of the graph are in millions.

Cultural indicators confirm that Pakistan as a whole, in its pace of historic development, still belongs to the Indian subcontinent and specifically to its northern part. It is close in many respects to Uttar Pradesh, Rajasthan, and Bihar. This situation can hardly be considered a surprise: Two of the major Indo-European languages of the north straddle borders. In the west, Punjabi is the language of the Punjab region of Pakistan and of the Indian state of Punjab; in the east, Bengali is the language of Indian West Bengal and of Bangladesh.

Dates at which the literacy threshold was crossed are close together. For men the level of 50 percent was reached in 1972 in Pakistan, 1975 in Uttar Pradesh, 1976 in Bihar, and 1979 in Rajasthan. For women, dates were equally close but reversed: 50 percent knew how to read in 1997 in Uttar Pradesh and Rajasthan, and in 2002 in Pakistan and Bihar. One might note a greater delay for women in Pakistan, but one should not lose sight of the fact that the region as a whole is one of those where the status of women is lowest on a planetary scale. In Hindu areas, there is a long tradition of the confinement of women, purdah. Gaps in female education are tending to increase. In 2005, 39 percent of university students were women, whereas in Arab countries and Iran, parity if not superiority in numbers of women was the norm.

The index of excess female mortality between the ages of 0 and 5 is 119, clearly higher than rates in the Arab world: 102 for Morocco, 106 for Yemen, 106 for Saudi Arabia, and 112 for Syria. But it is lower than those in the Hindu world: 143 in Uttar Pradesh, 140 in Rajasthan, 135 in Bihar, and 198 in Punjab! But Punjab, where Sikhs are the dominant religious group, is a region in the forefront, remarkable in its exceptionally favorable indicators of cultural development. The threshold of 50 percent literacy was crossed by men in 1961 and by women in 1981. On a regional scale, excess female mortality is moderated in Pakistan for a common reason in patrilineal systems: Pakistanis frequently marry their cousins. Women are protected by their life membership in a patrilineal group. Among the radically exogamous Hindus and Sikhs, women are transferred at marriage to other family groups. They are a burden rather than an opportunity for their birth family and are ill treated as a consequence. The case of Punjab reminds us that the decline in the fertility rate, which reduces the number of children and the chances of having a son, generally acts as an aggravating factor in excess female mortality. If the country is a modern one, ultrasound also makes selective abortion of female fetuses possible. China is close to Punjab, with an index of 184. Even in Pakistan, despite the protection of daughters by a 50 percent rate of endogamy (one of the highest in the Muslim world), a link between progress and the aggravation of the situation of girls can be observed. To appear modern, parents state in surveys that they are indifferent to the sex of the child. In reality, they get rid of daughters as much as they can. Selective feticide, made possible by ultrasound, is limited in the countryside, where the male ratio at birth of 106.4 is very little above the normal or natural level of 105. But in cities, the male ratio of 108.1 is above the norm.

DEMOGRAPHIC NORMALITY AND POLITICAL THREAT

Close in measures of cultural development to northern India, Pakistan is also close to the least advanced Arab countries, Yemen and Morocco. As in those two countries, the decline in the fertility rate slightly anticipated the access of the majority of women to literacy. The case of Pakistan is intermediary, because the first decline in the fertility rate occurred in 1990, 12 years before the literacy threshold was crossed. In Yemen, the advance was only 9 years; in Morocco, under European influence, it was 21. It would be interesting to study in detail the effects on Pakistani patterns of thought of the Iranian demographic transition to the west and of the lower fertility rates observable in northern India, despite comparable levels of development. The Hindus so close by had fertility rates between 3 and 4.

The Pakistani fertility rate is slowly declining: In 1988 it was at 5.56 children, and since then it has lost only 0.9 percent annually. With 4.6 children in 2005,[6] the Pakistani fertility rate, the highest in this group, is far above that of the Arab world, except for Yemen. One cannot fail to be impressed by the alignment of the fertility of the Muslims of northern India with that of Pakistan: In 1998–1999, it was 4.8 in Uttar Pradesh, 4.9 in Rajasthan, and 4 in Bihar. One might suggest a slight boost from the combined effect of minority status and the fact that Muslims in these states belong to the least privileged strata in social and educational terms. The minority effect must play the leading role, because elsewhere in India, in states where Muslims enjoy higher than average educational status, in Tamil Nadu and Karnataka, they also have a higher fertility rate than their Hindu neighbors (see table 6.1).

Pakistan is supposed to be homogeneous because 97 percent of the population is Muslim. It is in fact shot through with lines of division that aggravate the destabilizing effects of its demographic growth.[7] Islam is not a sufficiently unifying force to silence identity politics in a country that came out of two secessions. In these circumstances, the ideal of purity expressed in the name of the country might seem to be a dangerous defiance of reality. The fertility rate in the peripheral provinces and groups—Baluchis, Siraikis, Pashtuns—is higher than that among the

TABLE 6.1 Fertility and Illiteracy in Indian States by Religion

| | Fertility 1998–99 | | Illiterate Women (%) | |
	HINDUS	MUSLIMS	HINDUS	MUSLIMS
Uttar Pradesh	3.9	4.8	70	75
Rajasthan	3.7	4.9	76	81
Bihar	3.4	4.4	76	83
Madhya Pradesh	3.4	3.4	70	58
Haryana	2.8	6.0	55	89
Gujarat	2.7	3.1	52	40
Maharashtra	2.5	3.3	46	38
Orissa	2.5	3.0	60	55
Delhi	2.4	3.0	29	54
Punjab	2.3	3.3	35	64
Andra Pradesh	2.2	2.5	65	51
Tamil Nadu	2.2	2.6	50	35
Himachal Pradesh	2.1	3.2	35	66
Karnataka	2.0	2.8	56	60
West Bengal	2.0	3.3	46	61
Assam	2.0	3.5	50	64
Kerala	1.6	2.5	12	17

Sources: International Institute for Population Sciences, National Family Health Survey (NSH-2) India 1998–99: one volume per state, ORC, Macro, 2001.

central ethnic groups—Punjabis, Sindhis, and Urdu-speaking Muhajirs driven out of India after the 1947 partition. The taboo is so powerful in the "country of the pure" that, without apparent reason, the government postponed a census scheduled for 1981 to 1991, and finally carried it out in 1998. It was a matter of putting off delicate questions about the representation of ethnic groups in parliament and the resulting budget allocations, the resolution of which traditionally favored the central provinces. All of this oddly recalls the situation in Lebanon.

Another resemblance with Lebanon is the presence of Shiites, who make up 20 to 25 percent of the population. These 40 million individuals make Pakistan the second largest Shiite country in the world, after Iran. They are often subject to attacks from Sunni fundamentalists. The Sipah-e-Sahahba Pakistan party wants Pakistan to declare itself a Sunni state and for Shiites to become second-class citizens: another non-Muslim minority alongside the Hindus and Christians. The Shiites, pretransitional like their Lebanese co-religionists of an earlier period, have tried to protect themselves from these political risks by a defensive fertility rate, higher than that for other Pakistanis. They are, to be sure, poorer and less educated, but, like the Muslims in India, they suffer from a minority complex.

With a level of development close to that of the least advanced Arab countries, Pakistan is also the only Muslim country that is a nuclear power. It has paid very dearly for its technological advance: 6 percent of the GDP is devoted to defense, in relative terms three times that of India, if differences in population size are taken into account. This martial capacity, which cannot fail to bring about a certain militarization of society, partially explains the weakness of the state's efforts in the area of development.

The unspoken fact of Pakistani demography is rivalry with India. The Pakistani atom bomb is only one symptom among others, and perhaps not the most important one. Questioned about their view of their country's demography, Pakistani authorities tirelessly repeat that they find the fertility rate too high. This is a well-rehearsed refrain, composed and sung to satisfy the suppliers of funds: the World Bank, the IMF, and USAID. It is indeed worth asking whether the high fertility rate does not reflect the deep aspirations of leaders who are at bottom more concerned with geopolitical power relations in the subcontinent than with the well-being of their population. In the Sunni Arab world, the fertility rate floor below which the most patrilineal countries have not been able to fall is 3 children per woman. In Pakistan it is not yet certain that it will go below 4, even if it is too soon to assert that Pakistan is going to deviate from a trajectory matching its level of development. The situation is in fact worrying, whatever the scenario. Pakistan is in a period of demographic transition, and it is hard to predict the form an ideological and political transition to modernity might take in a country where the principles of patrilinealism and endogamy are exhibited in maximum terms. There will be an Islamist impulse, but how will it be expressed? With a little imagination, the breakup of a family structure made dense by a rate of endogamy of 50 percent might recall the disintegration of an atomic nucleus. If the anxiety of the United States in the face of Iranian nuclear ambitions appears to be exaggerated and in bad faith, the thoughtlessness manifested by American diplomacy in handling its Pakistani ally, a real nuclear power, seems to be frankly irresponsible.

AFGHAN PARENTHESIS

The porous border between Pakistan and Afghanistan has enabled the Taliban, most of whom are Pashtuns, to get from their Pakistani cousins all the military aid and moral support they needed to fight against NATO troops after their 2001 "defeat." Demographic growth among the Pashtuns is even more explosive than it is elsewhere in the region. All the ingredients are united to raise the fertility rate on the Pakistani side to regional records that prefigure those in Afghanistan. The age of marriage has been very low (16.8), particularly among the younger generations, and contraception has been very unpopular: 15 percent of couples used it in 2003, half the rate of Punjab, where it was not very frequent.

Afghan demography is not clearly understood, because of unremitting war: the Soviet invasion, civil war, and finally war with the Americans. Estimates by international organizations—largely hypothetical—nonetheless agree on a fertility rate of 6.80 children per woman and infant mortality of 146 per thousand, two variables whose values define the country as pretransitional. These assumptions are consistent with the country's underdeveloped state: 80 percent of the population is rural; the GDP is one of the lowest in the world; illiteracy is at 49 percent for men between 20 and 24 and 82 percent for young women. Men are, however, in the process of crossing the threshold of majority literacy, a moment likely to provoke ideological revival. Considering the previous military performance of the resistance, this figure should encourage extreme caution on the part of the Europeans and Americans in Afghanistan who are wondering how long they will be there.

BANGLADESH: OVERPOPULATION AND DECLINE OF THE FERTILITY RATE

Educationally, Bangladesh is even less advanced than Pakistan, making it one of the least advanced countries in the Muslim world. Men did not cross the threshold of 50 percent literacy until 1988, and women are not expected to do so before 2015. The evolution of the Bangladeshi fertility rate defies any cultural theory of transition, whether the classic theory of the driving force of female literacy, or, as in some Muslim countries such as Morocco, the theory that the same role is played by men. The fertility rate began to decline around 1970, 18 years before the majority of men could read and write. By 1995, the fertility rate had fallen to 3.25 children per woman. The change was swift, but it was followed by near stagnation: In 2005, the indicator seemed to have stabilized at 3 children per woman (see fig. 6.3).

The best response to such a theoretical challenge is a simple and reasonable one. Only an obvious and overwhelming factor can explain the unusual trajectory of Bangladesh. The astonishing density of the population (1020 inhabitants per square kilometer on average) suggests the hypothesis of an absolute overpopulation that led individuals to control their fertility before the effects of literacy kicked in, because no available space existed or was even imaginable. One might respond, correctly, that Egypt has no trouble reconciling one of the highest population densities in the world (2000 inhabitants per square kilometer) with a steady fertility rate. But Egypt can spread out on dry land, in the desert or along the Red Sea coast. It would be difficult to imagine Bangladesh building on water.

Bangladesh was until recently presented in Muslim countries as a model of demographic virtue for the speed of a transition accomplished despite its underdevelopment.[8] It is now a disappointment to development specialists and demographers.

The fertility rate is not the only measure that is no longer changing. Early marriage of girls has not really been challenged; the average age was 14.5 in 2004. Fifty-eight percent are married before the age of 15, and 85 percent are married before the age of 18. It would be unjust to attribute this practice to Islam, because child marriage was a tradition

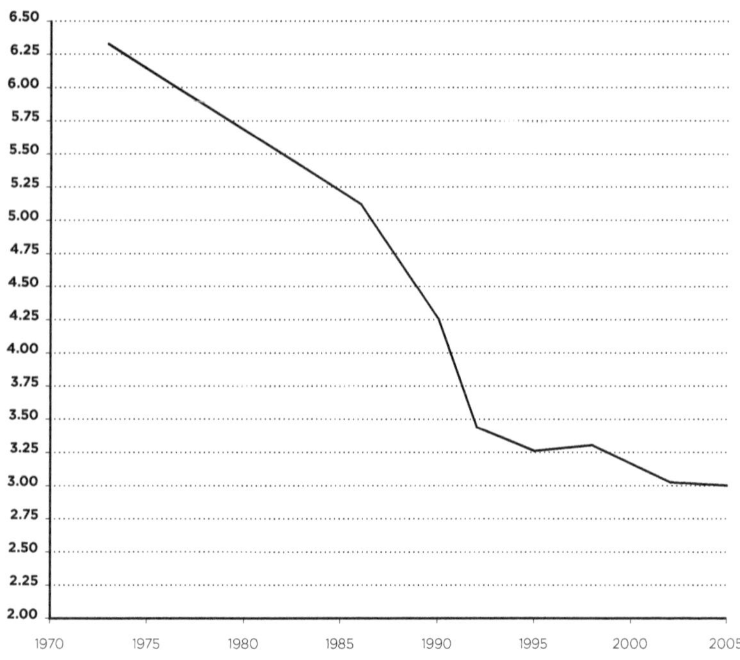

FIGURE 6.3 The stagnation of the transition of the fertility rate in Bangladesh, 1970–2005.

Sources: World Fertility Survey and Demographic and Health Surveys.

in northern India in general. Contraception, which is fairly widespread (58 percent of married women, 47 percent using modern methods, twice as many as in Pakistan), attenuates the effects of early marriage.[9] Abortion is rare, even though it is partially authorized. The desired fertility rate is much lower than the actual fertility rate: 2 children rather than 3. The status of women, although not very high, is still better than it is in Pakistan or in the neighboring area of northern India. Excess mortality of girls is not high: The indictor is 108 compared to 119 in Pakistan. The male ratio at birth (106 boys for 100 girls) does not show an excessive deviation from the norm.

Statistics convey contradictory messages about the condition of women. Schooling of girls before 15 is high: 78 percent, compared to 75 percent for boys. Early marriage subsequently blocks the advancement of girls, few of whom receive secondary and higher education. But wives sometimes work outside the home. The level of feminization of the work force is indeed not negligible, at 19 percent, twice as high as that in Pakistan. It is difficult not to draw from these data the impression that the family is a weak patrilineal system, associated with a rather low level of endogamy (8 percent), and the stagnation of the fertility indicator at 3 cannot be compared to what is sometimes observed in the Arab world: resistance by the patrilineal principle, the fear of not having a son.[10]

Nor is the ethnic dimension an explanatory factor. In Bangladesh, interethnic rivalries have little effect on the fertility rate, because the population is fairly homogeneous, although it is about 17 percent Hindu, Christian, Baha'i, and Ahmedi. All Bengali Muslims are Sunnis, except for a few tens of thousands of Shiites. Should the recent stagnation therefore be seen as the effect of a "return of Islam" in the strict sense, that is, in the luggage of émigrés returning to the country? Like Egypt and Syria, Bangladesh sends its émigrés to the Arabian Peninsula. They come back not only with consumer goods but also with a vision of Islam fostered by Wahhabism. This imported conservative Islam is said to explain, somewhat as in Egypt and Syria, the stagnation of the demographic transition. Mention is also sometimes made of a process of "Pakistanization," or even of "Talibanization" and the intrusion of political Islam into Bangladesh, since the defeat of the pro-Indian Awami League and the victory of a coalition between the nationalist party (BNP) and the Islamist Jamaat-e-Islami (JIB), incidentally led by a woman.

Some commentators have drawn attention to the divergent courses of the fertility rates in the two parts of Bengal. In Indian West Bengal, which is three quarters Hindu, the fertility rate is 2.07, below the replacement level. The contrast with Muslim Bangladesh, where the transition has been blocked, is striking. A shared language should have led to a convergence through cultural contagion, but a pietistic Islam seems to have frozen changes in patterns of thought in Bangladesh and, as a repercussion, provoked a halt to the transition. But a consideration of educational patterns leads to a rejection of the hypothesis of a direct effect of the religious variable on fertility. West Bengal has long enjoyed a much higher educational level. Men crossed the threshold of majority literacy as early as 1949, that is, 40 years before Bangladesh, and women crossed it around 1987, 28 years before Bangladesh. It is a little soon to attribute to Islam responsibility for the current stagnation of the fertility rate in Bangladesh, at a level that is not very high. We might on the contrary acknowledge that Islam has the virtue of not having prevented a rapid fall from 6.5 to 3 children per woman in a country that fulfilled none of the theoretical conditions for such a change.

ALONG AN AXIS RUNNING FROM THE BALKANS THROUGH THE Caucasus to Central Asia, a sort of contact line has been established between Islam, the newest of the great universal religions, and communism, the great universalist ideology of the twentieth century. The two beliefs were for a time superimposed on one another, usually because Russian or Yugoslav communism, a force from outside, politically controlled a piece of the Muslim world. In the case of Albania, however, the combination of communism and Islam was essentially an indigenous phenomenon: The pro-Chinese regime of Enver Hoxha was an authentic national creation produced in a country whose religion was Islam.

The existence of this long border, running from southeastern Europe to the heart of Asia, is not merely a matter of chance. Arab Islam and Russian and Serbo-Croatian communism have specific anthropological foundations, but they have some points in common and one fundamental difference, which is the origin of the border. The chief common point is a traditional family structure of a communitarian and patrilineal type, ideally associating the father and his married sons. The difference relates to the model of marriage, endogamous in the Arab world and exogamous in Russia and Yugoslavia. All the countries along the line of contact, whether Christian or Muslim, came out of a family development cycle that was communitarian and patrilineal. This is true for Albania, Bosnia, Serbia, Bulgaria, northern Turkey, the populations of the Caucasus, and all the populations of Central Asia, including the Uighurs of western China and, of course, the Chinese themselves, whether they are Buddhists, Confucians, or members of the Muslim Hui minority. The area of overlap roughly corresponds to the line of contact between endogamy and exogamy. But the distributions of the two models of marriage do not respect the division between Muslims and Christians. Some Islamized peoples, such as the Albanians of Albania and Kosovo, are exogamous, as are the Bosniaks, Chechens, Kazakhs, Kyrgyz, and Huis. The Turks of Turkey are endogamous, but at a rather low level. The Azeris are endogamous like the Turkomans, Uzbeks, and Tajiks. The Turkic-speaking peoples—Kazakhs, Kyrgyz, Azeris, Turks strictly speaking, and Uzbeks—do not all fit into the same category.

The cause of this distribution is hardly mysterious. The endogamous peoples are those who were the earliest Islamized, entering the sphere of the umma as early as the eighth century. The Islamization of the Turkic-speaking nomads is a relatively late phenomenon, extending from the tenth century to the thirteenth. Their clans were fiercely attached to the exogamy of the patrilineal group, and endogamy is frequent only where Turkic languages were adopted by Indo-European populations Islamized at an earlier date, particularly in Azerbaijan and Uzbekistan. The Tajiks retained their Persian, Indo-European language. The Muslim conquest of the Balkans is even more recent. It was carried out by the Ottomans, who were at first not strongly inclined toward endogamy. In the case of the Chechens, Islamization hardly goes back earlier than the eighteenth century. All the Turkic-speaking peoples were converted to Sunni Islam, with the sole exception of the Azeris, who came under the sway of Persian Shiism as the result of a complex history.

Azerbaijan, the homeland of Zoroaster and Zoroastrianism, was very early subdued by Muslim conquerors, almost at the same time as Syria and the Maghreb. In the thirteenth century the Turkish language was imposed by the Seljuk dynasty, but in the sixteenth the Azeris followed the Iran of the Safavids, broke away from orthodox Islam, and adopted the black banner of Shiism. It is the only people—the majority of them live in Iran—in this group in which Shiism dominates, including 75 percent of the population. Tajikistan is a kind of reverse Azerbaijan, Persian-speaking but Sunni.

We can study the combined demographic effects of Islam and communism in eight state entities: Uzbekistan (27.4 million population in 2007), Kazakhstan (14.8), Azerbaijan (8.5), Tajikistan (6.7), Kyrgyzstan (5.4), Turkmenistan (5.0), Albania (3.2), and Bosnia (3.9). We can add Kosovo (2.5), a well-defined territory, whose international status remains uncertain.

ACCELERATED INCREASE IN LITERACY

The proximity to Europe, the first center of literacy in the world, made the line of contact into a relatively advanced part of the Muslim world in terms of education. In the area of former Yugoslavia, the mechanisms of diffusion were facilitated by the fact that the three religions spoke practically the same language: Orthodox Serbs, Catholic Croats, and Muslim Bosniaks differed even less linguistically than in terms of family structure. Albania, whose language is Indo-European, but rather isolated, was surrounded by Christianized European countries that, although not making it a culturally advanced nation, made it possible to cross the threshold of 50 percent literacy for women between the ages of 20 and 24 around 1955. This was 65 years behind Greece and 25 behind Portugal.

In formerly Soviet Central Asia, European influence has been just as strong, but was not the result of a spontaneous form of dissemination. The Soviet regime had made mass literacy one of its priorities, and it fostered a remarkable acceleration of the process. Although it is not now fashionable to recognize the positive contributions of communism to human history, the fact remains that communism's sincere obsession with education greatly reduced illiteracy in Central Asia. The dates are uncertain, because Soviet censuses do not provide sufficient data. The last reliable census for literacy is that of 1926, a date when the threshold was far from being crossed. For example, Azerbaijan, an oil-producing region to which a large number of Russians emigrated, almost all of whom were literate, was certainly not the least advanced of all the Soviet Muslim republics. The literacy level of Turkish speakers between the ages of 20 and 24 was, however, only 25 percent for men and 4 percent for women, approximately the level reached by Syria around 1900. By the time of the next census in 1939, covering all the republics, the magic of Stalinism had already accomplished the impossible: simultaneous elimination of illiteracy for all generations, a falsification that subsequent censuses were not really able to correct. It seems reasonable to lower estimates of the results of Stalin's educational triumphalism and agree that men in the republics of Central Asia crossed the literacy threshold between 1940 and 1950 and women, between 1950 and 1960. This estimate would place the men of these countries immediately after those of Lebanon, that is, clearly in the front rank of Muslim societies.

Since the Soviet debates of the 1970s, we have been accustomed to recognizing the relative demographic backwardness of the Central Asian republics.[1] The Russians at the time were worried by the high Muslim fertility rate, which automatically introduced a new imbalance into the Union, in a situation in which the "Slavic" fertility was already much lower. At the end of the Stalin era and in the early years of Khrushchev, in the "Christian" part of the Soviet Union (Russia, Ukraine, Belarus, the Baltic countries), despite the ravages of World War II and despite natalist ideology, fertility had already fallen below 3 children per woman in 1950–1955. In the Muslim republics, which had been relatively spared during the war, fertility rates were twice as high, from 5.4 to 6.8 children per woman. Ironically, the Muslim republics seemed to be the only ones in the U.S.S.R. to adopt the Marxist anti-Malthusian norm of the time. Pro-Chinese Albania, having broken with the Soviet Union and Yugoslavia, did the same: 6 children per woman in 1958.

But if we change perspectives and situate the demographic history of Central Asia in relation to that of the Muslim world as a whole, we come up with an entirely different conclusion. The demographic transitions of Central Asia and the Muslim Caucasus occurred very early. In Azerbaijan, the fertility rate fell off around 1963, 20 years before Iran. The date was the same for Kyrgyzstan and Kazakhstan, although half the population of the latter was Russian. Fertility rates in Uzbekistan and Tajikistan fell off in 1973. Only Turkey, with a fall in 1950, and Tunisia, in 1965, had done better in the Muslim world. In most Arab countries, as we have noted, the transition began between 1985 and 1989. Even Turkmenistan, which brought up the rear, did better than the core of the Arab world, because its fertility began to decline in 1978. The dates indicating the beginning of the transition in the Muslim republics of the Soviet Union seem fairly compatible with our estimate for the decline in illiteracy among young women between 1950 and 1960. According to the standard theory of transition, this would be a classic case of female literacy causing a decline in fertility. At the western extremity of the zone of overlap between Islam and communism, in Albania, the standard theory works perfectly, because majority literacy for women reached around 1955 was matched by a first decline in the fertility rate around 1958. No delaying effect of Islam or of the patrilineal principle common to all these societies can be observed. Once literacy is achieved, a decline in the fertility rate follows. In all these countries except one, the current fertility rates show that the threshold of 3 children per woman has been crossed. In 2005, only Tajikistan was still at 3.40. Kyrgyzstan was at 2.87, Turkmenistan at 2.62, Uzbekistan at 2.43, the Kazakh population of Kazakhstan at 2.2, and Azerbaijan at 1.7. Albania's rate was somewhere between 2 and 2.15.

The average recorded total fertility rate for the former Soviet Muslim republics was 2.54, hardly higher than the average of 2.34 for the three countries of the Maghreb influenced by France. The comparison is logical and necessary. These two parts of the Muslim world experienced in parallel the massive influence of Europe in the form of French colonialism and Russian communism. The results were comparable: a notable advance over the rest of the Muslim world and an implosion of the patrilineal principle with the movement below the threshold of 3 children per woman. The exact mechanism of acceleration was not the same. Soviet action can in a sense be seen as classic. One simply needs to note that the acceleration of female literacy brought about an acceleration in the decline of the fertility rate. French colonialism did not have as positive an effect on literacy levels in the Maghreb as did communism applied to Central Asia. Educational levels in Algeria and Morocco were very low when France withdrew, and hardly any better in Tunisia. It is migratory movements and a cultural influence outside of education that largely explain the acceleration of the demographic transition in the Maghreb, especially in Morocco and Tunisia, where the fertility rate declined before women reached the 50 percent literacy threshold.

Azerbaijan is distinct for a particularly low fertility rate, markedly below the replacement level and closely resembling that of northwestern Europe. At 1.7, the country is close to many neighboring Iranian provinces, where in fact the majority of the Azeri-speaking population lives. Shiism encourages debate and rebellion against a world suspected of being unjust. It also shows traces of residual feminism. It is certainly responsible for the demographic modernity of Azerbaijan. The difference between the Sunni and Shiite branches of Islam in this case seems to be a more relevant explanatory criterion than the difference between the Muslim world and the Christian world. As for the border between the communized zone and the part of the Muslim world that remained "free," it has disappeared on the maps of fertility rates. But communism did leave its mark in very specific birth control methods that have nothing to do with modernity or gentleness.

UN-ISLAMIC BIRTH CONTROL: THROUGH ABORTION . . .

Where they are in closest contact with the West, in Lebanon and the Maghreb, women sometimes wait until they are 28 or even 30 to marry; a generation earlier they would have been considered old maids. Central Asia, on the other hand, is a kind of earthly paradise for women who want to get married: Less than 5 percent of Uzbek and Tajik women are unmarried at 30, 14 percent in Kazakhstan and Turkmenistan, 18 percent in Albania, and 24 percent in Azerbaijan.[2] In the Arab world that was under French influence, remaining unmarried at 30 is now customary; it is true of 41 percent of Moroccan, 54 percent of Tunisian, and 50 percent of Lebanese women. The record of 58 percent is held by Algerian women. The women of Central Asia marry young, between the ages of 20 and 21.5, and only from 1 to 5 percent never marry. Men do not marry women much younger than they are. In Uzbekistan, the age gap between spouses is only 2.7 years. The small age gaps clearly differenti-ate these countries from the core of the Muslim world, whether Arab or not. They point to a woman who is less of a minor and who has a higher status, and to a less absolutely patrilineal system. One can understand why the movement of the fertility rate below 3 was easy, because this breakthrough presupposes that 25 percent of couples have given up hav-ing sons, an attitude that signals the death of the patrilineal principle. It is not certain that this particularity has much to do with communism and its desire to emancipate women. A higher status for women in the context of a patrilineal clan system was typical of all the Turkish and Mongol groups on the steppes. Elsewhere, the Russian peasantry itself, well before communism, was characterized by a patrilineal system that preserved an abnormally high status for women and average age gaps between spouses that could fall to zero.

Left to itself, early marriage would produce high fertility. Birth con-trol therefore has to be carried out inside marriage. Far from taking ad-vantage of Muhammad's tolerance for coitus interruptus and Islam's tol-erance for contraception, Muslims of the former communist world use it very little and prefer abortion, which is condemned by Islam. This is a Soviet legacy. In Central Asia and Eastern Europe, resistance to mod-ern contraceptive methods reveals that the practice remains marked by the memory of the inferior quality of Soviet contraceptives, more seri-ous than for other products. Although the prevalence of contraception is increasing, it is doing so hesitantly. The rates are among the lowest in the world. In Azerbaijan, 33 percent of married women use some contraception (20 percent of them use a modern method); in Tajikistan, 27 percent; in Kosovo. 9 percent; and in Bosnia, 16 percent.

Most important, the habit has remained of the massive use of abor-tion, clearly inherited from the communist period. Sunni and Shiite Muslims sometimes hold different positions on dogma, but they agree in condemning abortion. At the International Conference on Population and Development in Cairo in 1994, the conservative Sunnis of El Azhar found themselves in agreement with the revolutionary Shiites of Iran in condemning abortion as a means of birth control.[3] But aside from Kosovo, Muslims were untroubled in taking full advantage of Soviet, Albanian, or Yugoslav legislation to reduce unwanted pregnancies. Abortion, widely practiced when the Soviet Union was culturally revolutionary, was prohibited by Stalin in 1936, but again authorized in 1955, a liberal measure that was part of the process of de-Stalinization. Soviet population policy, officially anti-Malthusian, had no fear of contradiction. With the halt in the distribution of contraceptives, abortion became the only method of birth control. Toward the end of the Soviet era, in 1988, the regulation of abortion was liberalized even further (extended to 28 weeks of pregnancy, authorized in case of widowhood, divorce, multiple birth, or rape). Central Asia and the Muslim Caucasus inherited what was becoming a tradition. In former Yugoslavia, the great liberalization of abortion in 1977 was not called into question by Bosnia once it was independent, nor by Kosovo. Even in austere Albania, the prohibition of abortion was evaded in practice. It was the contraception of the poor. Imported from the West, the pill and the IUD were reserved for the communist nomenklatura. Since then, Albanian legislation has been revised, and abortion has become the standard method of family planning.

Despite their incompleteness (there is always reluctance to declare a legal or clandestine abortion), figures reach extremely high levels. In Uzbekistan, for 2.4 children born, 1 fetus is aborted. The same is true of Tajikistan, Turkmenistan, Kyrgyzstan, and Albania. In Kazakhstan, the figures approach parity: 1.4 aborted for 1.9 born. The record for abortions is held by Shiite Azerbaijan, where there are annually twice as many abortions per woman as there are births: 3.2 compared to 1.7. Kosovo is an exception in this respect, because numbers of abortions there are negligible.

. . . AND THROUGH INFANT MORTALITY

Although not perfectly precise, figures on Wikipedia, taken from the CIA site, classify 226 countries according to their infant mortality, from the worst performance (Angola, with a rate of 187 deaths in the first year of life for 1000 live births) to the best (Sweden, at 2.8 per thousand). The ex-communist Muslim countries of Central Asia are among the worst. Tajikistan falls between Somalia and Mali, Azerbaijan between Laos and Benin, Turkmenistan between Haiti and Gambia, and Uzbekistan between Pakistan and Cambodia. Kosovo is close to Morocco and Cape Verde. Albania is in an honorable place between Venezuela and the Solomon Islands. Bosnia is the only ex-communist Muslim country that has a European statistical profile (see table 7.1).

The infant mortality rates of Muslim Central Asia are completely out of step with economic, social, and cultural indicators. Recent surveys such as the Demographic and Health Surveys provide more reliable values than the official record system inherited from the Soviet era, which is often deficient. They show, in contradiction to the universal law of decline, infant mortality is now increasing. In Azerbaijan, where the rate was 86 per thousand in 1989, it first declined to 74 in 1994, but went back up to 81 per thousand in 1999. It was still at 74 per thousand in 2005. The neighboring Shiite state of Iran at the same date had a rate of 31 per thousand. In 2005, rates in Central Asia ranged from 53 per thousand in Kyrgyzstan to 76 per thousand in Turkmenistan. The comparison with Arab countries is sadly significant. Central Asia was approximately at the level of Yemen. The Maghreb had rates between 20 and 40 per thousand, and the central Arab world, between 18 and 24 per thousand.

Rates of infant mortality are generally heavily dependent on a population's educational level. The former Soviet republics seem to have emancipated themselves from this law, because their cultural level has not prevented the persistence of very high mortality during the first year of life. To the extent that these countries seem quite capable of taking advantage of their cultural level to maintain a rather low fertility rate, the bad health record can only be the result of negligence that has some meaning. Shouldn't one see in these infant deaths a complement to birth control secured primarily through abortion? This interpretation does not mean that the authors of this book are opposed to abortion as such or that they approve the dogmatic and unrealistic attitude

TABLE 7.1 Rates of Infant Mortality per 1000 in 2005	
Tajikistan	76
Turkmenistan	76
Yemen	75
Azerbaijan	74
Kazakhstan	60
Uzbekistan	59
Kyrgyzstan	53
Kosovo	44
Morocco	40
Egypt	33
Algeria	32
Albania	24
Jordan	24
Saudi Arabia	23
Tunisia	20
Syria	18
Bosnia	10

Sources: Calculations based on national data, World Fertility Survey, Demographic and Health Surveys, PAPCHILD, PAPFAM, Gulf Surveys, birth registrations, population censuses.

of the Vatican to the subject. We are evoking a possible consequence of abortion Soviet-style, which was created by a politically violent society. This violence was clearly expressed, demographically and otherwise, by careless treatment of the human body. The figures of infant mortality in Central Asia reveal that the Soviet tradition has in this case been stronger than either Sunnis or Shiite Islam.

MUSLIM DIVERGENCES IN THE BALKANS

An investigation of the divergent demographic patterns of behavior of the Islamized populations of the Balkans—Bosnian Muslims and the Albanians of Kosovo and Albania—is an unforgiving exercise for anyone looking for some specificity of Islam as the origin of social behavior. Islam is in all these cases, of course, a strong marker of identity because it defines the ethnic or national group, sometimes, as for the Bosnians, even though a language does not enter into the definition. But beyond this contribution to ethnic identity, Islam seems to have had little effect, and one can interpret everything by relying on educational and linguistic variables, and the majority or minority position in the overall society. This is why there is no specifically Muslim demographic behavior in the Balkans. The Bosniaks, with a fertility rate of 1.23, seem to be a people of southern Europe among others. The Albanians, with 2 children per woman, are close to the French. The Albanians of Kosovo, or Kosovars, seem, on the other hand, to have come up against the floor of 3 children per woman, a level where they remain.

Before the 1992 war, the Bosnian Muslims,[4] converted Slavs, enjoyed a nefarious reputation in the Muslim world: not very observant, lovers of good food, pork, strong alcohol, and women in short skirts. They did not set great store by Ramadan, the five daily prayers, and the pilgrimage to Mecca. It has been said that the war fostered a return to Islam in society. The wearing of veils and beards is mentioned. It is pointed out that Islamists like Alia Izetbegovic, financed by Saudi Arabia, have come to power. Demographic data indicate nothing of the kind. On the contrary, fertility rates show a strong convergence between Bosnian Muslims and Orthodox or Catholic Slavs: Serbians, Croatians, Macedonians, and Montenegrins.[5] On the eve of the outbreak of the ethnic and religious conflicts, Muslims in Bosnia had a higher fertility rate than the Orthodox or Catholics. These fertility differentials changed the relative sizes of the various populations, a phenomenon that, as in Lebanon, played a role in the outbreak of civil war. It is also certain that the cultural crisis engendered by the final decline in fertility, as in Lebanon, contributed to the ideological disorientation of the population and to a rise in violence. But the current convergence of fertility indicators suggests, again as in Lebanon, the possibility of a regional society in which ethnic and religious tensions have been pacified (see table 7.2).

Kosovo is not supposed to have experienced a particular religious revival since the end of the war in 1999.[6] This lack has not prevented the

TABLE 7.2 Fertility Rates of Bosnian Muslims, Albanians, and Non-Muslim Slavs of Former Yugoslavia

Year	1932	1953	1961	1971	1981	2002
Muslims	5.47	6.68	5.68	3.10	2.60	1.23
Albanians		6.33	7.71	7.03	5.45	3.00
Non-Muslim Slavs	4.23	3.88	2.14	1.89	1.66	1.23

Sources: From 1932 censuses, surveys, birth registrations in former Yugoslavia. 2002: national data from Bosnia, Kosovo, Serbia-Montenegro, Croatia, Macedonia, and Slovenia.

continuation of divergent demographic behavior. The status of peripheral minority in relation to both the Serbs and the central Albanians is enough to explain Kosovar demographic dissidence.

Demography in Kosovo cannot be dissociated from history. In 1870, the date of the first census,[7] the population was only 60 percent Muslim (Albanians, along with a few Turks and Gypsies), with Orthodox Serbs making up the remaining 40 percent. One hundred thirty years later, in 1999, Serbs were only 10 percent and Albanians 90 percent of the population. The Albanian increase was not perfectly regular. Serbs sometimes tried to recapture the advantage by political means: During the Balkan Wars,[8] as in the interwar period, Serbs sought to colonize Kosovo to overturn its ethnic composition.[9] Between 1945 and 1964, Tito gave free rein to the anti-Albanian struggle conducted by his minister Marko Rankovic, who drove many Albanians, who were called Turks for the purpose, to go to Turkey. In 1999, the exodus of 700,000 Albanians during the Kosovo War might have lastingly reduced their presence in the province. The intervention by NATO decided otherwise. It is now the Serbs who are in danger of disappearing.

To confront the recurring threat of an environment that was at best hostile, at worst murderous, the Albanians' first line of nonviolent defense was their high fertility. This inclination toward large families did not escape their rivals' attention. As early as 1760, Patriarch Mazarek of Skopje described the Albanians as "the race that reproduces itself most quickly. A single family will create a hundred in a few years."

Two centuries later, the Serbian Major Arkan repeated the accusation and exhorted Serbs to have 4 children "to counterbalance the Muslim Albanians who breed like rabbits." The dominant demographic analysis of the time pointed to the foreign character of the Albanians: They were Asians, Turks, Muslims.[10] A transplant onto the Slavic body, a demographic aberration on European soil: "A European standard of living does not go together with an African birthrate."[11] The Yugoslavian demographer Milos Macura, director of the United Nations Population Division, explained this fertility from another era by the survival of the patriarchal family: The pressure of the social environment drives young people to marry early and have many children, all under the aegis of religious dignitaries. And indeed the fertility rates for the Albanians of Kosovo (6.5 children per woman compared to 3.4 for Serbs in 1961) were and remained high (3.40 children compared to 1.48 for Serbs before the 1999 war).[12]

These last figures point to a blocked demographic transition, with a fertility rate of 3.0 children per woman for Albanian Kosovars in 2003,[13] twice the Western average.

Data such as the large portion of the population that lives in rural areas (65 percent), and the fact that it is geographically scattered can account for the high fertility. Further, there is the high infant mortality of 44 per thousand. In short, the country is the poorest in Europe, with half of households living below the poverty threshold, a situation that is deteriorating, since per capita consumption declined in 2003 and 2004. Girls leave school too early, and illiteracy remains high, especially among women.

But underdevelopment is not the only causal factor. The twofold minority status of the Kosovars also played a role. The Serb threat was not the only question. The Kosovars also had to mark their difference from socialist, atheist, and modernist Albania, particularly with respect to the woman question. This sense of being under siege has not disappeared. If one compares fertility of Albanians in their different countries of residence, one is struck by the fact that it has not fallen below 3 children per woman where they are in the minority: in Kosovo, Macedonia, and perhaps in the Sanjak (in Serbia), Montenegro, and Greece. In Albania, where they are in the majority and secure, their fertility has fallen as low as 2.0 children per woman in 2005 (from 6.0 in 1958).

Among all the Muslims of Europe, the Kosovars are the least religious, the ones who are the least likely to put their Islam on display. They are also, considering cultural and demographic indicators, the most conservative. This is a paradox worth contemplating by anyone who would like to speculate about the demographic specificities of Islam.

THE SLOWING OF CERTAIN DEMOGRAPHIC TRANSITIONS RAISES a complex, almost metaphysical, problem of the ideal fertility rate that a country should reach in the aftermath of its transition: 2 children per woman, 1.5, 1, 0.5, 0? We set out this absurd sequence deliberately, the last figure of which points to the disappearance of the population in one generation, to make it clear that the very low fertility reached by Korea, Japan, Russia, Italy, and Germany cannot be considered as a reasonable and rational goal of every demographic transition. In a large part of the world, the transition has led to a dangerous imbalance, and many posttransitional countries should be looked at as examples not to be followed. But in expressing this opinion, we enter the uncertain and dangerous realm of values, in a more measured way, to be sure, than the religious systems that demand from their faithful as many children as the Almighty is willing to send them. A simple solution would be to define the replacement level as the goal to be reached: a fertility rate just above 2 in conditions of low mortality. But this would mean validating the Platonic dream of a society seeking, after removing the effects of age structure, to reach a stationary state considered optimal. This would be to dream of the end of history. In the France of the 1950s that had been humiliated by the Occupation and thought of its defeat as having something to do with its low fertility from 1900 to the 1930s, the rise of the total fertility rate to 2.6 in the course of the decade was considered an opportunity and as a manifestation of the society's will to survive.

Demography does not always manage to hide behind its mathematical tools the fact that its two subjects are also the subjects of religion: life and death. The recent evolution of Indonesia and several other countries of Southeast Asia, where fertility has noticeably declined but does not seem likely to fall below the replacement level, makes it impossible to dispense with this kind of question. Moreover, we are moving into a completely new area, where the stereotype of an Islam that is antifeminist by nature disintegrates. It will soon be clear that Indonesian and Malaysian fertility cannot be explained by recourse to the cliché of some Muslim specificity, and especially not by the notion of women's status being lowered by Islam.

It was noted earlier that the family structures of Muslim Indonesia and Malaysia widely deviated from the patrilineal, patrilocal, and patriarchal model that is often considered standard and is in fact dominant in the Middle East as a whole, whether Arab or not. In these Asian countries, which were Islamized late and peaceably, the wife's family predominates in social life, informally in Java, Malaysia, and the southern part of Sumatra. In the northern part of that large island, one can even find explicitly matrilineal systems. Mention should be made of the presence in Malaysia of a Chinese minority that adheres to a strongly patrilineal family system, and a moderately patrilineal Indian minority from the southeastern coast of the subcontinent.

The status of Muslim women in Indonesia and Malaysia is high. The birth of a girl is valued. The destruction of female fetuses, as in India or China, is unknown: The male ratio at birth is normal, 105 boys for

100 girls in Indonesia and Malaysia. Overt or hidden infanticide is unknown, and baby girls die less frequently than boys, a demographically normal phenomenon. Female schooling is complete, better even than that for males. The feminization of employment is high (38 percent in Indonesia, for example). Hiring of women in high-value-added sectors of industry and commerce is accelerating.

A NORMAL TRANSITION THAT HAS STOPPED

The Muslim countries of Southeast Asia are very unequal in size. Indonesia, with 228 million inhabitants, is a giant, the largest Islamic country in the world. Brunei, with 390,000, is microscopic, as are the Maldives, with 346,000. Second-ranking Malaysia, with 26 million inhabitants, is almost as populous as Morocco or Algeria.

The relative advance of these countries, educationally, demographically, and economically, would have led one to expect nearly perfect statistics. This is not quite the case. Irritating divergences show up, depending on sources, national or international. The question of bias then arises: Lower estimates of fertility and mortality present a better image of the country in the current ideological context, dominated internationally by the Anglo-Saxon Malthusian tradition. In the case of Indonesia, the rate of 2.28 children published by the United Nations Population Division points to a nearly completed transition; the rate of 2.60 children of the Population Reference Bureau suggests relative stagnation. Our estimate, based on an extrapolation from figures provided by Demographic and Health Surveys, suggests an intermediate level of 2.48. The question is not purely academic: Depending on the rate adopted, more than 400,000 births are added or removed. The fearsome law of compound interest warns us that from this choice flow widely divergent estimates of what the population will be in 20 years, in any event much more numerous in an exiguous territory.

The divergences are even more surprising in the case of Malaysia, because estimates of its recent fertility rate vary between 2.6 and 3.3. In the microstates, the situation of Brunei is fairly clear, with the number of children ranging from 2.3 to 2.6. The case of the Maldives transports us into a statistical world worthy of the *Thousand and One Nights*, with figures ranging, depending on the sources, from 2.7 to 5.0 children.

In terms of cultural development, despite its outlying position, Indonesia is one of the most advanced Muslim countries, flanked by Turkey and Jordan. The threshold of 50 percent literacy was crossed by men in 1938 and by women in 1962. This good performance certainly owes a good deal to the high status of women. The onset of the demographic transition fit the orthodox model, because it occurred around 1970, 8 years after the majority of women between the ages of 20 and 24 learned how to read and write. Malaysia was a little behind in literacy, because the decisive threshold was crossed only in 1958 by men and in 1972 by women, a very short gap of 14 years between the sexes. There seems to have been a principle of acceleration in operation, because fertility began to decline in 1965, even before the majority of women had become literate. But such brief intervals of time are not necessarily significant. This was still a standard transition associating female literacy and a decrease in fertility.

The subsequent history is more complicated, because the demographic transition seems to have come to a halt for the moment. Neither the economy, the educational level, nor the state of public health can explain the possible existence of a floor for fertility rate. Close to 2.5 for Indonesia, nearer 3 for Malaysia, a limit of this kind cannot in any way be motivated by the resistance of a patrilineal principle, which is absent from these regions. In Malaysia the fertility rate is above 3 children per woman, although schooling is universal, the GDP per capita is above $10,000, two thirds of the population is urbanized, and infant mortality, below 10 per thousand, is close to European levels.

Indonesia today might disappoint a Malthusian demographer. In 1997, one of the authors gave the chapter of a book the title "Indonesia: An Almost Completed Transition in the Largest Islamic Country."[1] Five years later, in 2002, the title was less definitive: "Indonesia: Transition in the Largest Islamic Country."[2] The slowing of the transition now leaves no doubt: 3 children in 1991, 2.9 in 1994, 2.8 in 1997, 2.6 in 2003, 2.5 in 2007. The decline is certainly continuing, but it is automatic, because of inevitable structural changes rather than as a result of the spread of innovative patterns of behavior. For example, the fertility rate for educated women is no longer declining and has stabilized at 2.5 children.

Why has this country, cherished by Malthusians, the favorite child of American family-planning programs, a model student of the World Bank and the IMF on demographic questions, stopped at the point when everyone expected another Japan (1.3 children per woman), South Korea, or Taiwan? The phenomenon is troubling. In addition to high status for women, Indonesia had every reason to continue toward a very low fertility rate. Population density is high, particularly on Java and Bali, in itself a spur to moderation. During the pretransition period, fertility was not that high, 5.67 compared to the 8 children found in Syria, Yemen, and Algeria. The will to master fertility was clear from the beginning: Indonesians adopted birth control even before infant mortality began to decline.

The technique used to master fertility was, to be sure, original. Universal and early marriage—age 19.2 for women on average and less than 2 percent permanently unmarried—did not produce too many children because it was countered by an extension of the period of breastfeeding, one of humanity's oldest methods for reducing the number of births. Breastfeeding in Indonesia lasts for almost 2 years (22.3 months). This natural birth control technique did not prevent the adoption of modern contraceptive methods by 60.3 percent of married women. Nothing suggested that there would be a slowing or eventual halt to the decline of fertility in Indonesia and Malaysia.

Indonesians have a specific behavior pattern. Regardless of background, age, social class, or educational level, they do not want the bare bones families of their rich Asian neighbors: The ideal figure considered as the key to happiness is 3 children, and the reality is more than 2 per woman.[3]

Is Islam involved? In Indonesia is it still the peaceable and syncretistic religion of past centuries? Religious tolerance was and remains more than a slogan to attract tourists. Like the faithful around the world, Muslims in Indonesia observe the proper rituals—daily prayers, the Ramadan fast, the pilgrimage to Mecca, alms-giving, and so on—but without excessive zeal.

But since the advent of the Islamic Republic in Iran in 1979, Indonesia has been and has felt itself to be closer to the central Muslim world, more in any event than at the time of Sukarno. The Gulf War of 1990–1991, the 2003 invasion of Iraq, and Israel's attack on Lebanon in 2006 had powerful repercussions. Although the Islamist attacks that have occurred since 2002 are isolated events, one may wonder about the increasing role of Islam in the state and in civil society. Measures that were unpopular in the past have been promulgated, such as the possibility of applying shari'a to marriage, divorce, inheritance, and the wearing of headscarves in public schools. The Muhammadiyah organization, an emanation of the Muslim Brotherhood, has 30 million members who make no secret of their intent to Islamize the country and revise legislation that they consider too secular. Recurrent sectarian unrest in Borneo, West Papua, the Moluccas, and Aceh recall the skirmishes between Muslims and Christians that have plunged the Nile Valley into mourning. And the war against the inhabitants of East Timor, 90 percent of whom are Christian, echoes the wars of religion of another era.

But Islam is not the key to all the problems. One need only compare the Indonesian archipelago, 90 percent Muslim, to the Philippine archipelago, which is 90 percent Catholic. The Philippine fertility rate of 3.4 children per woman exceeds that of Indonesia by one child, a good third. The geographical correlation between the fertility rate and the proportion of Muslims is negative in Indonesia (−0.4). On the less Muslim islands—Timor, West Papua, Sulawesi, Kalimantan, the Moluccas—fertility is much higher than on Muslim islands such as Java and Sumatra (see fig. 8.1).

More than religion, regional idiosyncrasies, with all they harbor of open or concealed resentments between demographic and political majorities and minorities, explain some excess fertility. Java, with 138 million inhabitants, largely dominates Sumatra, with 49 million. Larger and less densely populated than its neighbor, Sumatra has a higher fertility rate: 2.95 children per woman compared to 2.35 in Java. But all rates—standard of living, education, the status of women, and infant mortality—would have suggested the opposite. The differences are not

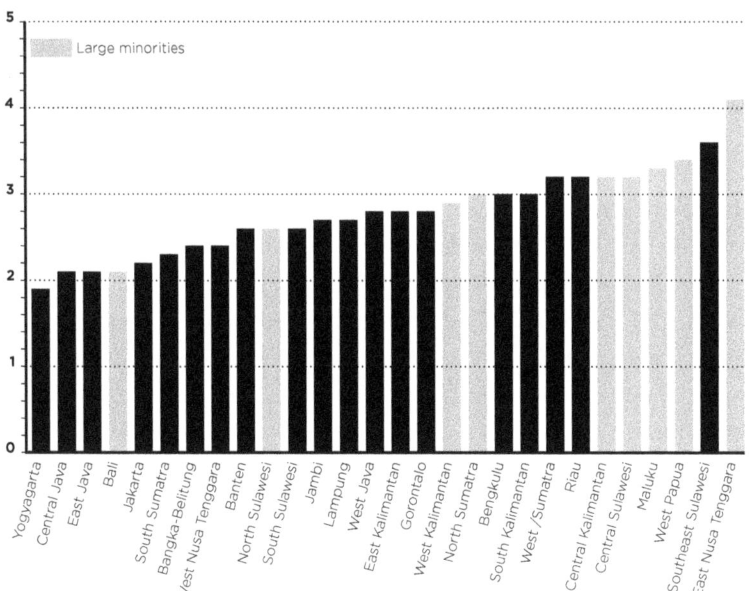

FIGURE 8.1 Fertility rates of Indonesian provinces (2002–2003) in relation to non-Muslim minority populations.

Sources: Badan Pusak Statistik, Indonesia, demographic and health survey, 2002–2003, ORC Macro, Calverston, Md., 2003.

religious, because they are all Muslims, apart from the Protestant Bataks of Sumatra and the Hindu Balinese of Java. Nor are the differences anthropological, because the overall levels of matrilocalism are comparable, except for the matrilineal Minangkabau province of West Sumatra and the patrilineal island of Bali. The Minangkabau are distinctly more Muslim than their environment and have a few more children, but they are also an archetypal minority whose faith is largely a matter of identity, as is their fertility.

Sumatra has for a century served as an outlet for migration, established during the colonial era by the Dutch rulers, but still used by the independent regimes dominated by Java. Two out of three of the transregional migrants settle in Sumatra. Threatened by this immigration, the inhabitants of Sumatra no doubt reacted with a higher fertility rate.

In neighboring Malaysia, fertility has also been mobilized to confront undesirable immigration.

IN MALAYSIA, NATIONALISM RATHER THAN ISLAM

In Malaysia, nationalism and fertility interact in Islamic costume. In the middle of the nineteenth century, the population was made up of a half million Malays (95 percent) and a handful of Chinese and Indians (5 percent). The low population density and the economic boom created by rubber and tin produced toward the end of the century a veritable gold rush. The British, who controlled Malaysia, encouraged the movement as sensible colonizers (divide and conquer) and as competent capitalists (put pressure on wages). By 1914, the Malays had become a fragile majority of only 57 percent of the population, compared to 29 percent Chinese and 10 percent Indian. The relative decline continued thereafter. By independence in 1957, they had lost the absolute majority, and Malays were now only 49.8 percent of the population.

To reverse the tendency, the new regime began by forging a nationalist ideology with an ethnic basis, *Bumiputera* (son of the soil), which provoked riots in 1969. A Chinese parade, more violent than the analogous Orange marches in Northern Ireland, was followed by a Malay counterparade. Preachers atop their minarets invoked the Muslim religion.

The NEP (New Economic Policy), a variety of positive discrimination, came next. It favored Malays, who were less represented in both the public and private sectors, through employment quotas. A "national" preference in favor of Malay companies was instituted for government contracts. Ninety-six percent of scholarships were reserved for Malay students. Malay became the exclusive language of instruction. Demography was not long in following this set of political, economic, and cultural reforms.

Malay Islam, traditionally mild and syncretistic, as in Java and Sumatra, was radicalized, transformed into a spearhead for a xenophobic nationalism. It is hard not to think of Ireland. Would Irish Catholicism have been so intense had it not been for the Anglo-Scottish Protestant invasion? Because it is by nature a collective belief system as much as it is a relationship to God, religion readily lends itself to ideological exploitation. A group's religious label can survive the disappearance of metaphysical belief. What can be seen in Malaysia is one of the most successful examples of the political exploitation of Islam; Malay identity has become consubstantial with Muslim religion. The word *Malay* is now a synonym of *Muslim*, as in the Ottoman Empire, when Turk and Muslim were equivalent, despite the existence of Christian and Jewish minorities who were just as Turkish. Islam has become a state religion, and conversion and apostasy are prohibited. Only the tribunals that apply shari'a have jurisdiction over personal status: marriage, divorce, polygamy, inheritance.

For Malaysian "Islamic supremacy" to assert itself, it needed a solid demographic foundation: more Malaysians, fewer Chinese and Indians. With respect to ethnic demography, Malaysia's policy was an unqualified success. Chinese and Indians of Malaysian nationality emigrated en masse, whereas the Malay population was increased by the immigration of ethnic cousins who came legally or clandestinely from Indonesia. But fertility played an even more important role than migration.

During the preceding century, the Chinese and Indians had more children than the Malays (see fig. 8.2). The fertility rate then declined, but more quickly for the Chinese and Indians. At the time of the ethnic riots of 1969, the gaps were still small: 5.1 children among Malays, 4.8 among Indians, and 4.6 among Chinese. Following the NEP and the increasingly ethnic character of ideological life, the Malay fertility rate stopped declining. Between 1970 and 1986, the modest movement from 5.1 to 4.8 children, accompanied by frequent fluctuations, was akin to stability, at a time when the Chinese fertility rate was declining by half and that of the Indians by a third. This is a clear illustration of the war of numbers, in a rather peaceable version compared to Palestine, Ireland, or Kosovo. The megalomaniacal national goal of "70 million Malays in 2100," twice the number that could be reached, had a partial effect. A fifth of Malays started having more than the desired number

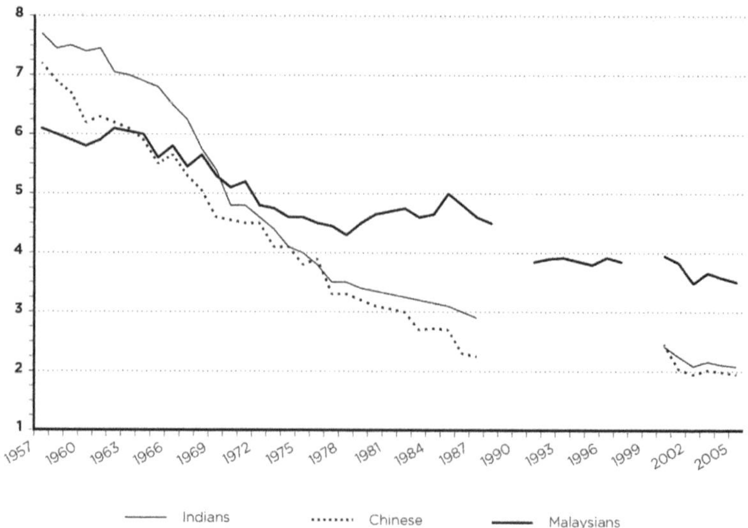

FIGURE 8.2 Ethnic/religious fertility in Malaysia.

Sources: Badan Pusak Statistik, Indonesia, demographic and health survey, 2002–2003, ORC Macro, Calverston, Md., 2003.

of children. Since 1986, the fertility rate has declined at a slow pace (1.3 percent annually on average). It was 3.5 children per woman in 2005, while the Chinese fertility rate of 1.95 had gone below the replacement level, and the Indian rate of 2.08 was hovering at that threshold. Unlike many Muslim countries where an economic crisis in or around 1985 was decisive in changing reproductive behavior, the Asian crisis of 1997 was not deep enough to cut into Malay natalism.

But the high fertility of Muslim Malays was also the result of their own aspirations. It was not imposed from above. A recent survey clearly shows that at equal educational and economic levels they have more children than the Chinese and Indians (+0.4), and twice as many of them want to have more children. Fifty-five percent of Malays do not use contraception, compared to 21 percent of Chinese and Indians.[4]

The high fertility rate of Malays is therefore not an effect of under-development. After four decades of positive discrimination, economic inequalities have become less marked or have even been reversed.

But Muslim Malays seem to have solved a rather improbable equation: high fertility in tandem with a proper status for women. It is true that the fashion for the headscarf, if not the chador, is spreading. But this is primarily a way of displaying Malay identity. Malay women enjoy much greater freedom of movement than Indian women do and play a considerable role in the job market.

According to the theoretical paradigm, Malaysia ought to have completed its demographic transition. In Singapore, where Malays are such a small minority that numbers have lost any political significance, their fertility has greatly diminished: It was at 2.07 in 2005, the replacement threshold.[5]

A detailed examination of Indonesian and Malaysian data does not validate the hypothesis of an Islam that plays a particularly active role in the demographic sphere. Questions of identity and confrontations between national, regional, and ethnolinguistic groups are, on the other hand, an obvious factor maintaining fertility at a level higher than the replacement threshold. The parallel sketched with the Catholic Philippines might open up a new and vast interpretive field that would place the family system at the center of the analysis. Common to Indonesia, Malaysia, and the Philippines is the mechanism of "temporary coresidence" of newlyweds with their family of origin. They continue to live for a few years with the parents of one or the other spouse, until the birth of the first child, or the marriage of the next brother or sister. In the Muslim regions considered here, usually the wife's family is the one involved. In the Philippines, it can be either the wife's or the husband's. There appears to be a similar mechanism in Latin America—in Mexico and Peru—but preference goes to the husband's family. Might there not be a connection between a fertility rate stabilized at around 2.5 children and this mechanism of temporary coresidence, which facilitates reproduction by guaranteeing to the young couple substantial, but not oppressive, family assistance at a crucial time? The Latin American countries mentioned above do not contradict this hypothesis. For the years 2000–2005, Mexico had a fertility rate of 2.4, and the majority of young women had learned to read and write by 1930. In Peru, the corresponding figures are 2.9 and 1950. We are not drawing any conclusions but merely suggesting that the question of maintaining fertility rate around 2.5 children goes well beyond Islam. With the temporary coresidence of newlyweds, we are confronted with a possible mechanism for maintaining the fertility rate that makes one think more of the effect of French daycare centers, in part responsible for the maintenance of the fertility rate at 2, than it does of a mysterious action of religious belief.

9/SUB-SAHARAN AFRICA

Sub-Saharan Africa is today the only continent where
fertility levels have remained high almost everywhere and where the
demographic transition is in its early stages. It is the continent of mass
polygamy, but in contradiction to a common stereotype, this form of
marriage is not the source of the African "demographic explosion." It is
true that achieving a high level of polygamy necessitates large age gaps
between spouses and therefore a very early marriage age for women,
which implies a long reproductive period. But some of these young
women are married to old men, whose sexual potency and fertility have
faded. Moreover, residential separation, which is frequent in polygamous families, does not foster frequent sexual relations.

One finds in Africa, however, all the usual correlates of demographic underdevelopment: a low standard of living, incomplete urbanization, and high infant mortality. But, as always, the best predictor of

fertility is the level of literacy, which remains lower than elsewhere despite rapid progress. Writing is not an ancient practice in Africa. If one sets aside the religious use of Koranic Arabic just south of the Sahara, before European colonization the continent had no system of writing. The process of catching up took place at a perfectly normal rate, but the backwardness in terms of literacy has not yet been overcome. This delay is general, but with nuances, common to the Muslim and non-Muslim regions of Africa.

Sub-Saharan Islam was the result of a relatively recent expansion. Although some African countries can be considered clearly Muslim (Mali, Senegal, Niger, Guinea, Gambia), others are characterized by unstable balances, such as Nigeria, Burkina Faso, Chad, and Guinea-Bissau. In the latter countries, the proportion of Muslims hovers around half the population. It is difficult to characterize other countries not considered in this book where the proportions, still imprecise, are not far from parity, such as Eritrea, Ethiopia, and Tanzania.

The pace of the eradication of illiteracy makes it possible to explain the greater part of the delay in the African demographic transition, particularly in Muslim regions. The threshold of majority literacy was crossed by men only around 1990 in Senegal, and was achieved in 2006 in Burkina Faso; it will be crossed in Mali only around 2010. For the women of these three countries, the threshold is yet to be crossed, with dates ranging from 2010 for Senegal to 2020 for Burkina Faso and Mali. Further south, in the partially Muslim countries Nigeria and Ivory Coast, literacy is more advanced. The rate of 50 percent literacy among men between the ages of 20 and 24 was reached by 1970 in Nigeria and Ivory Coast, and among women in 1983 and 1988, respectively.

In Nigeria, fertility began to decline around 1983, exactly when women crossed the majority literacy threshold, a clear illustration of the standard theory of demographic transition. But in Ivory Coast, Senegal, Burkina Faso, and Mali, we are once again confronted with a decline in fertility that anticipated female literacy: the decline was contemporary with or immediately following majority literacy among men between the ages of 20 and 24. In Mali and Burkina Faso, even the decline in

	% Muslims	Infant Mortality	Fertility
Senegal	94	61	5.26
Mali	90	113	6.75
Gambia	90	73	5.10
Guinea	85	91	5.71
Niger	80	123	7.55
Sierra Leone	60	163	6.49
Chad	51	102	6.32
Nigeria	50	100	5.59
Burkina Faso	50	91	6.20
Guinea-Bissau	50	116	7.09

Source: Table in the Appendix.

male illiteracy seems insufficient to explain the declines in fertility that occurred around 1990. Should we invoke the increasing population density, as in Bangladesh, or an independent action of the ties with France established by migratory flows? Considering that fertility indexes remained above 6, it is hard to draw conclusions from these transitions that have hardly begun and remain uncertain.

In the Muslim countries of sub-Saharan Africa, the average national fertility rate has reached 5.9 children per woman. At its lowest level in Senegal and Gambia, it exceeds 5. It reaches or exceeds 7 children in Niger, Mali, and Guinea-Bissau. As an explanation, one can immediately exclude a specific and massive effect of religion. In the non-Muslim countries of West, East, and Central Africa as a whole, fertility is at the level of 5.6 children per woman. The difference is thus only 0.3, on the order of 5 percent, a variation of little significance (see table 9.1). This is especially true because West Africa, where the majority of completely Muslim countries are concentrated and where fertility is indeed a little higher, was a strongly patrilineal area long before the arrival of Islam.

A lower status for women, independent of the Muslim religion, seems to be a much more important factor than religion to explain the relative excess fertility.

From this point of view, the case of Burkina Faso is the most typical. The population is only 50 percent Muslim, but of all the countries of West Africa it is probably the closest to the epicenter of the original African patrilinealism and polygamy. The partial character of the country's Islamization has hardly made it deviate from the rest of the region with respect to most parameters, notably fertility.

REGIONAL DIFFERENCES IN FERTILITY: ETHNIC GROUPS AND RELIGIONS

Nigeria, Burkina Faso, and Chad have Muslim majorities along with Christian and increasingly small animist minorities. These three countries show large regional differences in fertility, which make it possible to weigh the effects of Islam on fertility in particular contexts.

Very largely Muslim and even Islamist, northern Nigeria, where shari'a has been imposed in some states, has a higher fertility rate than the rest of the country: 7.0 children per woman in the northeast (dominated by the Kanuri), 6.7 in the northwest (Hausa and Fulani), and 5.7 among the populations of the north central region. These rates are clearly higher than those of the southeast and southwest: 4.1 children (Yoruba, Edo, Ibo, and Ekoi), or the south, with 4.6 children, populated primarily by Christians and Vodun practitioners, or both together. Careful research has shown a specific effect of the Muslim religion on fertility in Nigeria. Protestants and Catholics are more favorably disposed toward modern contraception, and Protestants' fertility is 20 percent lower than that of Muslims, and Catholics' fertility is 30 percent lower. Muslims also have a marked preference for large families.[1] But is this effect of Islam on fertility in Nigeria not due to the specific circumstances of the country and to a pure regional phenomenon? The denominational balance is precarious, recalling in some respects countries discussed earlier, such as Lebanon and Malaysia. Although it occurred 40 years ago, the Biafran secession, tinged with ethnic and religious separatism, brought about more than a million deaths and has not been entirely forgotten.

In addition, differences in fertility rates match an exceptionally large difference in literacy rates. In the southern provinces, the literacy levels of women between the ages of 20 and 24 was already between 60 and 90 percent in 1991. In the north, those rates ranged from 20 to 45 percent. The Yoruba in the southwest have been partially Islamized, although no educational and demographic impact of Islam is really measurable.

In Ivory Coast, ethnicity, religion, and fertility are intertwined, against the backdrop of the economic and identity crisis that followed the death of longtime President Félix Houphouët-Boigny. The debate about Ivoirian identity, which implicitly rejected the Muslims of the north, was also based on a demographic substratum. The Muslims of Ivory Coast, who made up more than 35 percent of the population and were bolstered by Muslim immigrants from neighboring countries (primarily Malinke), have a fertility rate of 6.2 children, more than 50 percent higher than the 4.1 of Christians; animists are in an intermediate position, with 5.6 children. But as in Nigeria, the difference in fertility is based on a difference in literacy rates. The language of the colonizer—French or English—arrived in the south, with all the impact of European culture. It is of course there that the highest literacy indicators can be found, along with the lowest fertility indicators. Without going into detail, it is also the case that the family systems of coastal regions, in very diverse styles, have all accorded a higher status to women from a time well before Islamization.

Just as multidenominational and multiethnic, but much more peaceable, Burkina Faso does not exhibit differences in fertility according to religion as large as those in Nigeria and Ivory Coast. Outside the capital of Ouagadougou, fertility is lowest (5.4) in the south center, populated by Gourounsi and Mossi, and highest in the Sahel region in the north (7.7), with a Fulani population. Although few Burkinabés call themselves animists (15 percent) and the great majority have chosen Islam (56 percent) or Christianity (29 percent), traditional religion remains influential. Fertility depends little on religion. The fertility of the Fulani in the north is high, but it derives from their nomadic or seminomadic way of life more than from their past as zealous propagators of Islam. Burkina Faso is not a coastal country and does not have the north-south regional stratification of levels of development of Nigeria and Ivory Coast.

Chad is a sort of miniature Sudan or Mauritania, with nonblack Muslim ethnic groups, such as the Toubou and Fulani in the Sahara and Sahel regions of the north, and black Christian or animist populations in the south. Historically, the north, land of the overlords, made up of former sultanates, dominated the south, the *dar-el-abid*, land of the slaves. Fertility differs according to religion, but in exactly the opposite way from what is seen in Nigeria: The Christians and animists of the south are more fertile (6.5) than the Muslims of the north (6.2). The south, which is more developed, should have had lower fertility. For example, female illiteracy, which is at a high 61 percent in the south, reaches a record of 94 percent in the north; for men the rates are 21 percent in the south and 84 percent in the north. One must therefore point to Christian excess fertility and not exclude the hypothesis of a political component to the phenomenon, due to the troubled history of this composite country.

MUSLIM GIRLS SPARED BY MORTALITY

The demographic scourge of sub-Saharan Africa is not so much its high fertility level as its record levels of infant mortality and adult mortality from AIDS. African mortality follows an atypical model. It is high, of course, before the age of 1. But contrary to the general norm, it remains high until the age of 5. In sub-Saharan Africa, children from 1 to 4 die as much as they do before the age of 1, sometimes, as in Niger, 40 percent more. One child out of four or five dies before age 5, and it is normal in a sense that sub-Saharan fertility is high to counterbalance the effects of that mortality.

Are Muslim girls even more the victims of this situation than boys? Excess female mortality in childhood (between birth and age 5) appears in half the Muslim countries: Nigeria, Senegal, Niger, Burkina Faso, and Chad. But excess female mortality among sub-Saharan Muslims is lower than in North Africa and on other continents, in the Middle East, the Caucasus, and Central Asia. In addition, in 14 out of 24 non-Muslim countries in sub-Saharan Africa, excess female mortality is higher than in the Muslim countries.

At first sight, Islam seems to provide good protection against the AIDS that is ravaging sub-Saharan Africa, provoking considerable declines in life expectancy in peacetime. The "Christian" countries have been most harshly affected: 20 percent of the population infected with AIDS—with a peak of 33 percent in Swaziland—in the sexually active age groups. Life expectancy has fallen below 35 in southern Africa, where there are few Muslims. On the other hand, the ten Muslim countries have avoided the pandemic: fewer than 4 percent of individuals infected in the worst-hit countries—Nigeria, Chad, Guinea-Bissau—and 1 to 2 percent in the other countries. The most likely explanation probably has to do with greater control over female sexuality in the West African countries, where Muslims are concentrated. But, independently of Islam, mention must also be made of more patrilineal family systems before attributing a better health situation to greater religious and moral rigor.

For now, sub-Saharan Islam remains quantitatively in a minority position. Although it has more Muslims than the former Soviet sphere, it is far behind Arab, other Middle Eastern, and Southeast Asian Islam. Only one Muslim out of six is a sub-Saharan black. But a shift of the demographic center of gravity is already present in the uneven levels of fertility. Where an "ex-communist" or Southeast Asian Muslim now has only a little more than 2 children, an Arab or other Middle Eastern Muslim has 3.5 (and that level is precarious because of the speed of transition), the rate in Muslim black Africa has remained close to 6 children. The powerful inertia of demographic movements guarantees that in the course of the twenty-first century there will be a displacement of the center of gravity of Islam toward the south. It is not impossible that one day the fundamental problem associated with Islam will no longer concern its relations with the "Christian" or "post-Christian" north, but the upending of its internal balances.

CONCLUSION

DOES ISLAM INFLUENCE DEMOGRAPHY? ON THE BASIS OF THE historical and geographical survey of the preceding chapters, the answer is clearly no. The spectrum of Muslim rates of fertility around the world—from 1.7 to 7 children per woman—is as varied as the types of Islamic believers, from agnostics and atheists to militant fundamentalists and Salafis, taking in along the way the flourishing category of those who are simply "sociologically" or "culturally" Muslim. Muslim unity, unchanging Islam, and Muslim essence are imaginary constructs.

When Islam has had an independent effect on demographic transition, this has been deliberately exaggerated. In view of the number and power of other variables, emphasis on Islam as a causative factor is primarily a symptom of intellectual myopia. Literacy, patrilinealism, reactions of minority groups, and oil wealth all reduce the idea of Muslim demographic specificity to the level of a residual variable.

This does not mean eliminating the religious phenomenon from the analysis. It does mean rejecting the notion of Muslim, and for that matter, Christian specificity—for religion has been shown in this book to be fundamental in two respects, one broad and one narrow.

Broadly, all religions are openly or implicitly natalist because they provide meaning to life. This is why the undermining and fading of religion, along with increasing literacy, seem to be conditions for a fertility decline. In this respect, nothing distinguishes Islam from Christianity.

The narrower religious issue relates to the difference between the Shiite and Sunni variants of Islam. It is relevant in that it makes it possible to interpret the low fertility of Iran, Azerbaijan, the Shiite areas of Lebanon, and the Alawite areas of Syria. There is no doubt that if peace is restored and statistical surveys become possible, there will be a demographic split between Shiites and Sunnis in Iraq. Religion is important in these circumstances, but only to the extent that it articulates a particularity within Islam. The split between Catholicism and Protestantism was an explanatory element of the same order. Contrasts like this, useful in interpreting certain statistics at a given time, are not permanent. They shed light on delays, temporal gaps, but are not indications of an eternal separation. Until the early twentieth century, there was a strong contrast between Catholicism and Protestantism. Max Weber used it in his analysis of the culturally and economically advanced position of the Protestant world. But it has lost relevance and no longer helps account for European economic and demographic diversity. The same thing will happen for the division between Shiites and Sunnis.

To understand the modernization of Europe, we have to be able to envision a long cycle in which the growth of literacy, de-Christianization, and subsequent decline in fertility at first accentuated differences between religious zones and then led to convergence. An analogous picture must be used to understand the modernization of the world as a whole, or rather the extension of the process of modernization of ways of thinking that affected Europe before other continents. The Muslim world is now at the center of the transition to modernity. The fertility rates of some countries have already caught up with those of Europe. Others are barely beginning their evolution. But the process is so clearly under way that we cannot avoid speculating about the emergence of a unified world. Human societies will never be entirely alike, and it would be absurd—and sad—to imagine a world that was homogeneous in every detail. The beauty of Europe resides largely in the persistent differences between Sweden and Italy, between England and Hungary. Demographic analysis of societies can obviously not replace the analysis of cultural differences, but it sets a limit to what is intellectually acceptable in that analysis.

To accept the optimistic conclusion of this book that runs against conventional wisdom, one must of course be aware of the efficacy of the demographic variable. It is necessary to imagine the extent to which it affects the private life of man and society. Perhaps we are asking the reader to adopt a strange belief about a dimension he may never have taken seriously. But by accepting the postulate of the decisive importance of birth control as a driving force of modernity that sheds light on the evolution of patterns of thought, we can avoid the sinister image of a planet divided into civilizations closed off from one another, composed of populations made different by their religions. There was a time when analysts theorized about the emergence of a *homo sovieticus*, different in essence from Western European and American man. But at the same time, the collapse of the Russian fertility meant that Russians were men like other men. The appearance of freedom of choice in sexual and family life could not fail to be followed by an extension of this same idea of freedom to ideological and political life.

Today there is a great temptation, in a world made anxious by economic globalization, to classify, separate, and, of course, condemn. Some powers and some researchers have an interest in fostering the image of a conflict of civilizations, which masks the latent violence of economic conflicts. Demography can free the mind from this easily exploited paranoia and makes it possible to go further. The populations of the world, with different forms of civilization and religion, are on converging paths. The convergence of fertility rates makes it possible to imagine a near future in which the diversity of cultural traditions will no longer be seen as a source of conflict but will simply be evidence of the richness of human history.

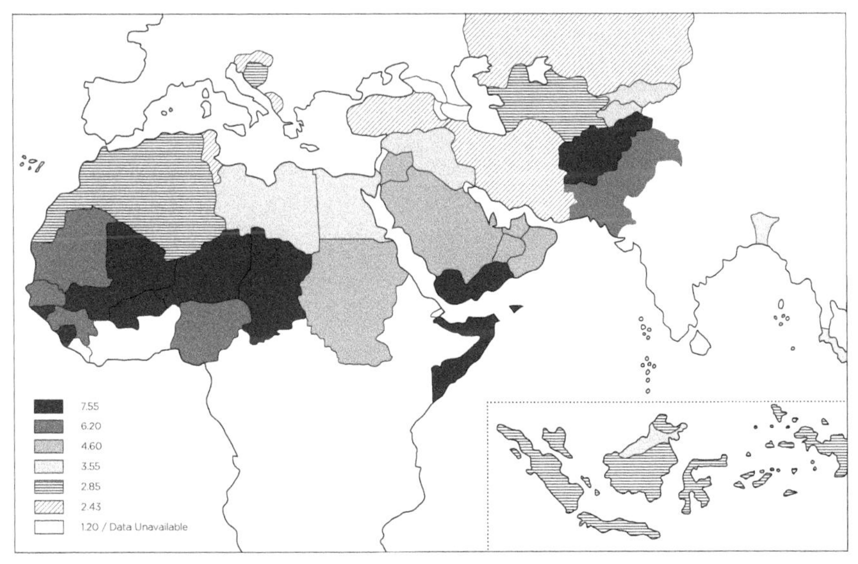

APPENDIX MAP Total fertility rates of Muslim Countries.

APPENDIX TABLE Demographic and Socioeconomic Indicators of Muslim Countries (Muslim population 50% or higher)

	Population in 2007 (thousands)	Percent Muslim	Fertility Rates in 2005	Maximum Fertility Rates	Year	Rate of Infant Mortality (p. thousand)	Literacy Rate, Young Men (%)	Literacy Rate, Young Women (%)	Percent Urbanized
ARAB COUNTRIES									
Morocco	32784	99	2.43	7.40	1972	40	81	61	55
Algeria	33861	99	2.57	8.36	1962	32	94	86	49
Tunisia	10312	98	2.02	7.25	1962	20	96	92	65
Lybia	6085	97	2.85	7.62	1982	24	98	97	86
Mauritania	3247	100	5.20	6.79	1987	71	68	56	40
Egypt	76853	94	3.36	7.07	1962	33	90	79	43
Sudan	37793	70	4.20	6.67	1972	64	85	71	36
Iraq	30291	97	3.50	7.30	1957	88	89	81	68
Syria	19988	94	3.50	7.80	1982	18	94	90	50
Jordan	5966	96	3.55	8.00	1967	24	99	99	82
Lebanon	3653	60	1.69	5.74	1948	17	99	99	87
Palestine	2867	96	3.70	8.00	1962	21	99	99	57
Sudia Arabia*	25809	100	3.61	8.45	1976	23	96	96	86
Yemen	22325	100	6.20	8.70	1982	75	59	44	26

United Arab								
Emirates*	4775	100	3.69	7.50	1982	9	93	93	74
Kuwait*	2839	100	4.14	7.50	1962	10	100	100	96
Oman*	2668	100	3.56	8.70	1986	10	98	97	71
Qatar*	857	100	4.44	7.75	1972	9	95	98	100
Bahrain*	751	100	3.10	6.21	1972	10	97	97	100
Somalia	8766	100	6.23	7.25	1962	119	45	34	34
Comoros	841	98	5.09	7.05	1982	59	91	80	33
Djibouti	820	94	4.20	7.80	1962	99	79	55	82

GREATER NON-ARAB MIDDLE EAST

Turkey	75161	99	2.35	6.90	1953	39	98	93	59
Iran	71220	98	2.00	7.00	1963	31	99	97	67
Afghanistan	32254	99	6.80	8.00	1998	146	51	18	20
Pakistan	164594	97	4.60	6.60	1983	79	76	55	34
Bangladesh	147059	83	3.00	6.85	1963	65	86	82	23

EX-COMMUNIST COUNTRIES

Uzbekistan	27371	88	2.43	6.80	1963	59	100	100	36
Kazakhstan	14802	56	1.89	4.56	1958	60	100	100	57
Azerbaidjan	8536	93	1.70	5.64	1963	74	100	100	52
Tadjikistan	6682	90	3.40	6.83	1973	76	100	100	26

continued

APPENDIX TABLE (*continued*)

	Population in 2007 (thousands)	Percent Muslim	Fertility Rates in 2005	Maximum Fertility Rates	Year	Rate of Infant Mortality (p. thousand)	Literacy Rate, Young Men (%)	Literacy Rate, Young Women (%)	Percent Urbanized
EX-COMMUNIST COUNTRIES									
Turkmenistan	4965	89	2.62	6.75	1963	76	100	100	47
Kirghistan	5386	75	2.87	5.39	1963	53	100	100	35
Albania	3163	80	2.15	5.98	1958	24	99	99	45
Kosovo	2500	90	2.71	5.65	1954	44	98	90	33
Bosnia	3920	52	1.20	4.82	1953	10	100	100	43
SOUTHEAST ASIA									
Indonesia	228121	90	2.48	5.67	1958	34	99	99	42
Malaysia	26240	65	3.07	6.94	1958	10	97	97	62
Brunei	390	67	2.60	7.00	1958	9	99	99	72
Maldives	346	100	2.73	7.00	1978	15	98	98	27
SUB-SAHARAN AFRICA									
Nigeria	137243	50	5.59	6.90	1983	100	84	68	44
Mali	14325	90	6.75	7.56	1983	113	38	25	30

Senegal	12218	94	5.26	7.00	1983	61	67	48	45
Niger	14907	80	7.55	8.15	1998	123	40	27	21
Guinee	9808	85	5.71	6.80	1983	91	69	36	30
Burkina Faso	14042	50	6.20	7.68	1988	91	46	29	16
Chad	10303	51	6.32	6.65	2003	102	52	34	24
Sierra Leone	5802	50	6.49	6.50	2003	163	59	37	36
Gambia	1594	90	5.10	6.50	1983	73	85	79	50
Guinee Bissau	1682	50	7.09	7.10	2003	116	59	37	48

Sources: Calculations based on national sources, birth registrations, censuses, and various *Surveys*: World Fertility Survey (WFS); Demographic and Health Surveys (DHS); Pan-Arab Project for Child Development (PAPCHILD); Pan-Arab Project for Family Health (PAPFAM); and the following works: United Nations, *World Population Prospects as Assessed in 2006* (New York, 2007); U.S. Census Bureau, *IDB Data Access Spreadsheet, 2006*; Population Reference Bureau, *World Population Data Sheet* (Washington, 2006); Youssef Courbage, *New Demographic Scenarios in the Mediterranean* (Paris: INED, 2002).

When the proportion of Muslims was not provided by national data (censuses, surveys, etc.), they were determined with the help of various websites and, if necessary, the CIA site, The World Factbook: https://www.cia.gov/library/publications/the-world-factbook/index.html.

* Indices, except population, are for nationals, omitting foreigners.

Chapter 1. The Muslim Countries in the Movement of History

1. Two classic works on the march of literacy make it possible to measure and to sense the irregular and irresistible character of the process. For Europe and the United States: Carlo M. Cipolla, *Literacy and Development in the West* (Harmondsworth: Penguin, 1969). For France: François Furet and Jacques Ozouf, *Reading and Writing: Literacy in France from Calvin to Jules Ferry* (Cambridge: Cambridge University Press, 1982).

2. Note that the correlation coefficient varies between -1 and +1 and that the connection between two variables is stronger as the absolute value of the coefficient approaches 1 and weaker as it approaches 0.

3. To assess the degree of variation explained by the correlation, the coefficient has to be squared. A coefficient of +0.84 explains 71 percent of the variation. A coefficient of 0.55 suggests that only 30 percent of the variation in the date of the decline in fertility is statistically explained by the coming to adulthood of the first generation of literate women.

4. Youssef Courbage and Emmanuel Todd, "Révolution culturelle au Maroc: Le sens d'une transition démographique," *Res Publica*, February 2007.

5. In the sense Max Weber gives this expression: the decline of religious and magical beliefs as a way of explaining phenomena.

6. A detailed study of these very precise chronological coincidences can be found in Emmanuel Todd, *L'Invention de l'Europe* (Paris: Seuil, 1990), chapters 4 (literacy), 6 (de-Christianization), and 7 (birth control). On the role of de-Christianization in the spread of birth control, see also Ron Lesthaeghe and Christopher Wilson, "Modes of Production, Secularization, and Fertility Decline in Western Europe, 1870–1930," in *The Decline of Fertility in Europe*, ed. Ansley J. Cole and Susan Cotts Watkins (Princeton: Princeton University Press, 1986), 261–92.

7. Joseph M. Kitagawa, *Religion in Japanese History* (New York: Columbia University Press, 1966), 226.

8. Abdou Filali-Ansari, *L'Islam est-il hostile à la laïcité?* (Casablanca: Le Fennec, 1997) and Mohammed Tozy, "La Méditerranée à l'épreuve des enjeux religieux," in *La Méditerranée au XXIᵉ siècle: Visions prospectives* (Casablanca: GERM, 1997).

Chapter 2. Crises of Transition

1. Christian Baudelot and Roger Establet, *Suicide: The Hidden Side of Modernity*, trans. David Macey (Cambridge: Polity Press, 2008), 23–35.

2. Lawrence Stone, "Literacy and Education in England, 1640–1800," *Past and Present* 42, 1 (1969): 69–139.

Chapter 3. The Arab Family and the Transition Crisis

1. N. J. Coulson, *Succession in the Muslim Family* (Cambridge: Cambridge University Press, 1971), ch. 8, "Inheritance in Shi'i Law," 108–34.

2. The sex ratio designates the number of men in the population per 100 women.

3. Christian Baudelot and Roger Establet, *Suicide: The Hidden Side of Modernity*, trans. David Macey (Cambridge: Polity Press, 2008), 42.

Chapter 5. At the Heart of Islam: The Arab World

1. Dudley Sirk, "Factors Affecting Moslem Natality," in *Family Planning and Population Programs*, ed. Bernard Berelson (Chicago: University of Chicago Press, 1966).

2. There was a lower fertility rate in Mauritania and Sudan because of conjugal instability (the influence of sub-Saharan Africa), frequent absence of the husband from the household, polygamy (residual elsewhere), prolonged breastfeeding, and female excision, a cause of sterility.

3. Except for the rhythm method, which fits in well with the Christian preference for abstinence.

4. We are reluctant to place Palestine in this group because, even though its fertility rate is still 3.7 children, the decline in fertility since 2000 has been staggering.

5. Philippe Fargues, *Générations arabes: l'alchimie du nombre* (Paris: Fayard, 2000), 81–110.

6. The second transition did not begin until 1989. The pioneer of the Arab world was one of the last to set out on the path of transition.

7. In these circumstances, fertility rates found in international sources don't mean much because they are clouded by the large presence of foreigners (whose fertility rates are very low). For this reason only figures for the national populations are presented here.

8. The Twelver, Zaidi, Ismaeli, and so on, Shiites are about 15 percent of the Saudi population.

9. A little lower according to the U.N. Population Division (5.93), much higher according to the U.S. Census Bureau (6.67), and 6.20 children in 2003 according to a scientifically conducted PAPFAM survey.

10. Lebanese living in Lebanon in 2005 were divided into 31.5 percent Shiites, 29 percent Sunnis, 5.5 percent Druze, 19.9 percent Maronites, 5.0 percent Greek orthodox, 4.2 percent Greek Catholics, 3.6 percent Armenians, and 1.3 percent other Christians. If the Lebanese diaspora is taken into account, the proportion of Christians increases, because more of them have emigrated.

11. C.-F. Volney, *Travels Through Syria and Egypt in the Years 1783, 1784, and 1785* (London: G. & J. Robinson, 1805).

12. In special clinics, Hezbollah has assumed complete responsibility for very costly programs to fight sterility and support in vitro fertilization, theoretically open to the entire population.

13. In comparison, in Morocco, where there was no conflict, the fertility of university graduates (1.7 children) fell beneath the replacement threshold.

Chapter 6. The Non-Arab Greater Middle East

1. Marie Ladier-Fouladi, "Démographie, femme et famille: relations entre conjoints en Iran post-révolutionnaire," *Revue Tiers-Monde* 182 (April–

June 2005), and Amandine Lebugle-Mojdehi, "Lorsque les zones rurales rejoignent les zones urbaines: la baisse de la fécondité dans les villages de l'Iran," *Les Lundi de l'Ined*, March 2006.

2. Marie Ladier-Fouladi, "Démographie, femme et famille."

3. Emmanuel Todd, "Les États-Unis sont plus dangereux que l'Iran pour la paix," interview by Philippe Cohen, *Marianne*, October 7, 2006.

4. With the exception of the repression of the Baha'i.

5. All Arab countries are centralizers, like the Jacobins, and tend to blur the ethnic and linguistic dimensions of demography. Morocco is a notable exception in this respect: It dared to ask about and publish in its last census in 2004 data on the Amazigh (Berber) language.

6. Since birth records are deficient, we have to rely on surveys. The latest Pakistani surveys in 2001 (4.03) and 2003 (3.93) provided rates lower than that of the Population Reference Bureau used here: 4.60, the same as that proposed by the World Bank (4.5). The U.N. Population Division (4.0) and the U.S. Census Bureau (4.14) provide a lower Pakistani fertility rate. But our demographic analysis (based on the ratio of children to women in the last survey) showed that the rate of 4.6 was more probable.

7. Although one should not take too seriously separatist impulses like the creation of an independent Sindh or the secession of Karachi, a city of 15 million where the Muhajirs are in the majority, which would become a kind of Hong Kong.

8. The level of deprivation in the country is not as well illustrated by the abstract data of national statistics as by concrete observations: Three quarters of households do not have a radio, for example.

9. Breastfeeding, which lasts almost to the age of 3 (32.4 months), among other things, allows Bangladeshi women to regulate their fertility, which has not exploded despite early marriage.

10. Disparities between desired and actual fertility are high in Bangladesh, and cast doubt on the sincerity of those surveyed. We therefore rely more in facts than intentions.

Chapter 7. After Communism

1. They were a source for Hélène Carrère d'Encausse, *Decline of an Empire*, trans. Martin Sokolinsky and Henry A. La Farge (New York: Newsweek Books, 1979).

2. Curiously, the figure is 33 percent for Kosovo, for circumstantial reasons.

3. Circumstantial allies of the Vatican and delegations from conservative Catholic countries for this purpose.

4. Sometimes called Bosniaks; the word Bosnian is applied to nationals of the Republic of Bosnia-Herzegovina, whatever their ethnicity or religion.

5. Youssef Courbage, "Demographic Transition among Muslims in Eastern Europe," *Population*, an English election, vol. 4 (1992), pp 161–86. *Population* 46, 3 (1991): 651–77.

6. For the recent influence of islam in Bosnia, see Xavier Bougarel, "Travailler sur l'islam dans la Bosnie en guerre: Partie 1," *Cultures et Conflits* 47, 3 (2002): 49–80, and on patriarchal society and Islam in Kosovo, Jean-Arnault Dérens, *Kosovo, année zéro* (Paris: Éditions Paris-Méditerranée, 2006).

7. Conducted by the Austrians.

8. Leon Trotsky, a war correspondent in the Balkans at the time, asserted that the Serbs, "in their national endeavor to correct data in the ethnographical statistics not quite favorable to them, are engaged quite simply in systematic extermination of the Muslim population." *The War Correspondence of Leon Trotsky: The Balkan Wars 1912–13* (New York: Monad Press, 1980), 286.

9. The attempt failed because Serbs rose to only 38 percent of the population, whereas their aim was 68 percent, according to the plan for ethnic cleansing. Vaso Cubrilovic, "The Expulsion of the Albanians," in Robert Elsie, *Gathering Clouds: the Roots of Ethnic Cleansing in Kosovo and Macedonia* (Peja: Dukagjini Balkan Books, 2002), 97–130.

10. It is noteworthy that fertility is what best brings out differences and fosters fantasies by emphasizing unlikeness. The adversary is stigmatized by emphasizing the human swarm, women constantly pregnant, and children crowding towns and villages.

11. *Politika*, October 30, 1988, quoted by Michel Roux, *Les Albanais en Yougoslavie: Minorité nationale, territoire et développement* (Paris: Éditions de la Maison des Sciences Humaines, 1992), 332.

12. But the fertility of Albanians never reached the level of 8 children per woman that it did in other Muslim countries such as Syria, Algeria, and Mali. It was cut in half (from a crude birthrate of 46 per thousand in 1954 to 25 per thousand in 1998) despite a political context not very favorable to demographic changes. In a political context of resistance through demography and a war over fertility, one might have expected the opposite, an increase or a constant fertility.

13. The direct factors that explain this high fertility rate are the relatively low marriage age of 24.2 (compared to 28 to 29 in the Maghreb), and the infrequent use of contraception, 32 percent compared to 65 percent in the Maghreb. Abortion is not unusual among the Albanians of Kosovo, but its frequency is unknown.

Chapter 8. Matrilocal Asia

1. Youssef Courbage, "L'Indonésie: une transition presque achevée dans le plus grand pays d'Islam," in *La Population du monde: Enjeux et problèmes*, ed. Jean-Claude Chasteland and Jean-Claude Chesnais (Paris: INED/PUF, 1997), 183–208.
2. Youssef Courbage, "L'Indonésie: la transition dans le plus grand pays d'Islam," in *La Population du monde: Géants démographiques et défis internationaux*, ed. Jean-Claude Chasteland and Jean-Claude Chesnais (Paris: INED/PUF, 2002), 244–64.
3. The ideal number 3 corresponds to 2.9 surviving children declared, taking account of infant mortality. One can also take into account the synthetic rate of desired fertility, which gives the lower figure of 2.2 children.
4. Philip Morgan et al., "Muslim and Non-Muslim Difference in Female Fertility: Evidence from Four Asian Countries," *Population and Development Review* 28, 3 (September 2002): 515–37.
5. But higher than the Chinese rate of 1.08, and that of the Singapore Indians of 1.25, both of whom are committing demographic suicide.

Chapter 9. Sub-Saharan Africa

1. Muyiwa Oladosu, "Prospects for Fertility Decline in Nigeria: Comparative Analysis of the 1990 and 1999 NDS Data," United Nations Population Division Workshop on Prospects for Fertility Decline in High Fertility Countries (New York, 2001).

GPSR Authorized Representative: Easy Access System Europe, Mustamäe tee 50, 10621 Tallinn, Estonia, gpsr.requests@easproject.com

www.ingramcontent.com/pod-product-compliance
Ingram Content Group UK Ltd.
Pitfield, Milton Keynes, MK11 3LW, UK
UKHW040318121125
464974UK00001B/3